JUDSON PRESS
PUBLISHERS SINCE 1824

Praise for Peggy Kendall's *Connected: Christian Parenting in an Age of IM & MySpace*

"I love this book because it gives practical advice on how to build these bridges between Gutenberg people and Google people. Instead of the customary narrative of cultural decline, expressions of cultural anxiety, denunciation of the awfulness of the times, not to mention millennial moanings, what Peggy Kendall gives us are strategies for passing the baton onto succeeding generations without the trade of tirades."—From the Foreword by author, speaker, and professor, Leonard Sweet, Drew Theological School, George Fox University

"If we blink, the technology changes. How's a parent to keep up? Dr. Peggy Kendall provides the answer with this wonderfully practical and useful book. If your kids are on the Internet, this is a must-read."—David Walsh, PhD, President, National Institute on Media and the Family and author of *No: Why Kids—of All Ages—Need It and Ways Parents Can Say It*

"Highly recommended for parents everywhere." —*Midwest Book Review*

Connected: Christian Parenting in an Age of IM & MySpace won a 2008 **iParenting Media Award for Outstanding Products.** These are comments from the reviewers:

"I believe this book opened the doors between my child and myself in reference to the Internet. We can now agree on the surfing, MySpace, and really understand and acknowledge the trust we have in each other." —iParenting Media Awards reviewer

"I like how the author used things from her own life and experience. I found the book easy to read and entertaining. I also thought the 'Get Connected' bits throughout each chapter and 'Good discussion starters' were helpful. It's a great way to really get the parents involved." —iParenting Media Awards reviewer

"Well written, up to date, and quite informative. It was nice to read a book that was focused on the spiritual positive and negative aspects of technology." —iParenting Media Awards reviewer

Praise for Peggy Kendall's *Rewired: Youth Ministry in an Age of IM & MySpace*

"I appreciate the approach taken in this book because it is thoughtful and measured—not too 'gee whiz' and not too jihad. Peggy Kendall talks about both the dangers and the benefits of cyber-relationships... Perhaps the most important facet of this book is that Peggy Kendall knows something about real, live teenagers. The stories she tells remind us that this book is not just a research project, nor is it even a book about the Internet. It's primarily a book about kids and those who care about them, and about how those of us who are youth pastors and parents can redeem the Internet as a place for community, learning, and building faith. It's a very cool idea, laid out very well, in a very good book." —Duffy Robbins, professor of youth ministry, Eastern University

"For the older youth minister, it's a direct way to figure out how to respond to what might be a frustrating trend, and for the young minister who already is deeply involved in this, it's a good resource for understanding the pitfalls." —Darrell Pearson, professor of youth ministry, Eastern University

"This book will be a helpful resource for classes on youth culture, youth ministry programming, or evangelism." —Eduardo M. Ramirez, associate professor of youth ministry, Eastern University

"*Rewired* takes what for many of us is a confusing and overwhelming world—the world of adolescent online communication—and walks us through it, deftly explaining and broadening our understanding. Kendall has written an engaging and straightforward book, providing in-depth analysis of social networking—how-tos, implications, and ideas for how social networking can be a positive experience for teens, concluding each chapter with a concise glossary of terms and ideas. A must-read for today's parents and youth workers." —Pamela J. Erwin, professor of youth ministry and practical theology, Bethel University, and board chair, Association of Youth Ministry Educators

"Rewired is culturally 'right on' and biblically sound. Recommended for youth workers." —*Church Libraries,* Summer 2008

Reboot
Refreshing Your Faith in a HIGH-TECH World

Peggy Kendall

Foreword by Robert Parham

JUDSON PRESS
PUBLISHERS SINCE 1824
VALLEY FORGE, PA

Reboot: Refreshing Your Faith in a High-tech World
© 2010 by Judson Press, Valley Forge, PA 19482-0851
All rights reserved.

Judson Press has made every effort to trace the ownership of all quotes. In the event of a question arising from the use of a quote, we regret any error made and will be pleased to make the necessary correction in future printings and editions of this book.

Unless otherwise indicated, Bible quotations in this volume are from the from HOLY BIBLE: *New International Version,* copyright © 1973, 1978, 1984. Used by permission of Zondervan Bible Publishers.

Library of Congress Cataloging-in-Publication Data

Kendall, Peggy.
Reboot : refreshing your faith in a high-tech world / Peggy Kendall. -- 1st ed.
    p. cm.
Includes bibliographical references (p.   ).
ISBN 978-0-8170-1565-7 (pbk. : alk. paper)   1.   Technology--Religious aspects--Christianity. 2.   Christian life. I. Title.
BR115.T42K45 2009
261.5'6--dc22
2009037604

Printed in the U.S.A.
First Edition, 2010.

To Jay, Nate, Aaron, and Hannah, my best buds

Contents

Foreword

One of the best ways to bring balance to our hyperdriven lives in a technologically over-connected and manically entertained world is to read *Reboot*. This book will slow down our multitasking long enough for us to think about how we conform to a technology-centric society and how we could transform our technology use to approximate more closely the living of authentic Christian faith.

Reboot: Refreshing Your Faith in a High-tech World is anything but another thinly veiled, quasi-negative book about technology salted with biblical proof-texts and preachy admonitions. Reboot isn't about disconnecting. It's about staying connected the right way. It's about making sure that the operating system of our lives runs the way it should without freezing up or crashing altogether.

Technology is a given—and it is given its rightful due by author Peggy Kendall, associate professor of communication studies at Bethel University in St. Paul, Minnesota. She clearly has no interest in returning to the days before computers and cell phones.

"When technology enhances our ability to multitask on many levels, we clearly gain some pretty impressive things. Put plainly, we gain an ability to get more things done," she writes. "Seriously, I would not want to go back to the days of my Selectric typewriter and little bottles of Wite-Out correction fluid.... I shudder when I think of a time long ago when I had to wait until I got home to find out what I was supposed to have picked up at the grocery store. I like being able to do things efficiently when the situation demands. I like being able to spend time with my kids or my husband even when we aren't near each other."

Kendall recognizes that technology can be a pro-family tool. At the same time, she understands the limits of technology. "One of the things that we tend to lose out on is participating in the here and now," she laments.

Noting Jesus' capacity to be in the moment, Kendall warns, "When technology pulls us to disengage with the people and the world around us, that is when we need to intentionally choose to take the time to be present in the here and now before we miss what was there and left."

Herein is one of the key messages of *Reboot:* In a high-tech, fast-paced world, we need to make good choices that ensure balance and enrich our lives as people of faith. At times, those choices might require a "technology Sabbath" or "technology fast"—a time to disconnect for a day, a week, or even forty days. Whenever and however we hit the pause button in our techno-centric world, part of that spiritual "reboot" should be a closer connection to God and a greater awareness of technology's role in our daily lives.

Kendall has written an easily readable book with a good working structure, weaving in relatable personal stories. She recalls memorable segments from TV programs such as the Andy Griffith Show and Alias. She clicks through different technological tools and turns to biblical texts.

Readable should not be confused with simple, however. *Reboot* is not a simple book. It is a challenging one for readers who accept the dominant role of technology in their lives without reflecting on what that hardwiring of technology to human beings does to social creatures. For example, *Reboot* underscores both the benefits of technologically-based relationships—for example, social networking—and the sacrifices that result from them.

Reboot deserves the attention of three distinct groups of readers. First, many local church clergy will profit from reading *Reboot,* especially seasoned clergy whose latest use of technology is limited to cell phones and email. They will get a refresher course on the variety of ways their congregants use technology. Equally important, they will begin to think about what technology may do to the moral character of people of faith. That recognition will require church leaders to frame technology theologically, inviting congregants to abandon assumptions that technology is either morally neutral or spiritually harmless.

Second, young adults will benefit from studying *Reboot,* and not only those who are college students taking communications courses.

Granted, communications students at Christian colleges should be connecting their academic discipline with their faith. But all young people of faith need to consider the relationship between their faith values and technological choices.

Third, Bible study groups and church-sponsored book clubs will find *Reboot* a rewarding read, especially if members are tentative about technological innovations. They will gain a sense of how younger church members might be using technology—why that technology makes their lives easier and gives them a sense of being more connected to community. They, too, will begin to think theologically about technology.

Whether you fall into one of the three groups named above or not, I think this book will help Christian technology consumers make better choices—choices informed by faith.

Read *Reboot*. Refresh your faith.

Robert Parham
Executive Editor
EthicsDaily.com.

Acknowledgments

I would like to thank my many students and colleagues at Bethel University who helped me sort through the questions of technology and faith that I have addressed in this book. My Communication, Technology and Society class was especially helpful in providing outrageous examples and never letting me stop with the easy answers. I would also like to thank my family for providing an unending stream of interesting things to write about. What would I do without you?

Introduction

As the sun peeks through the white-laced curtains fluttering in the morning breeze, the smell of frying bacon seeps into the bedroom. Beaver rolls over in his cuddly bed with the cowboy sheets.

"Gee-whiz," he thinks, "this is going to be a great day!" He quickly throws on his best jeans and T-shirt and runs downstairs for breakfast.

"Good morning, Beaver," says his dad, Ward Cleaver, as he turns the page of the morning paper. His mother quickly places a plate full of scrambled eggs, bacon, and toast in front of him and gives him a kiss on the cheek. She goes back to the stove, where she is dishing up a plate for Wally, who has joined the other men at the table.

Just like every morning, June Cleaver is dressed in a comfortable dress with high heels and, of course, her signature pearl necklace. Her hair still has that bounce in it from the curlers she slept on. As she begins cleaning up the breakfast dishes, she thinks about what she will do today. After some vacuuming, she probably will stop by the Rutherfords' house for a cup of coffee. She likes to keep up on what is happening around town. As with any day, June Cleaver is a mother with focus and drive. Her focus is on her role as wife and mother, and her drive is to provide a well-organized, well-sanitized, highly nutritious experience for her family.

The Cleavers' life seems so slow—simple, really. They talk to each other, and they eat real food. Dad might solve an occasional problem with Beaver, but he always takes the time to reassure his wife that it will be okay. Now, I know that real life probably was a little different back in the 1950s than what we saw on *Leave It to Beaver*. There were conflicts, people had to wash dishes by hand, kids got hurt, and there weren't many opportunities for women outside of the local garden club. Still, life seems fundamentally

1

different sixty years ago. Compare the average Cleaver morning to the average morning at my house.

I wake up early to spend twenty minutes with my friend Kathy Smith, the workout video woman. We have a good time together because Kathy always tells me I'm doing a good job and never comments on how flabby things seem to be looking. Soon my husband is up. He wanders into the kitchen and pops up his laptop to read the morning headlines. My two kids, after being cajoled to rise from their beds, stumble into the kitchen. One plugs ear buds into his iPod, and the other quickly sits down to check for any e-mail and instant messages she might have missed since she logged off late last night. The table is quiet while we eat our respective cereals, all except for a faint snap, crackle, and pop, the clicking of keyboards, and a muffled beat emanating from the ear buds. Before my daughter finishes her chocolaty cereal, she texts her friend about what she is wearing and heads out the door. We let the dog out, and soon everyone else is out the door, each hopping into his or her respective car. We won't see each other again until the after-school soccer games begin, my husband and I traveling between the two.

The afternoon and evening in my family is more of the same. As I pull up to watch a soccer game, I text my husband to pick up a pizza on his way home. I cheer on my daughter in between cell phone conversations and quick ducks into my car to finish some work from the office. By the time I get home, half the pizza is gone, my son is off to a church activity, and my daughter is planted in front of the TV with her laptop in one hand and the remote in the other. She's ready to start her homework. By the time my family falls into bed at night, we have seen each other for only a short time and have spoken real-life words and eaten real-life food together even less. Keep in mind that each of us has been involved in lots of good and important things throughout the day. We have been efficient and productive, but we have spent almost no time looking into each other's eyes, listening to what we have to say, sharing the precious moments we might have together as a family.

The Hyperdrive Trade-off

There is a change that has taken place over the past fifty years. It seems that somehow the speed of American life has jumped into a kind of overdrive. As we become hyperconnected, overstimulated, multitasked, hyperinformed, hectically scheduled, and manically entertained, we wonder why we feel so tired at night. Our hyperdriven lives certainly allow us to accomplish and experience more than ever before, but it's quite possible that this modern lifestyle also has caused us to sacrifice more than we realize. Unfortunately, the thing we need most to examine those sacrifices is the thing we seem to have the least ability to spare: time to stop and think.

When we make the choice to kick it into overdrive (and I would contend that it is a choice), there's no doubt that we gain things and we lose things. The things we gain are clearly laid out for us on the software box, in the cell phone plan, or in the employment contract. Time-saving technology gives us the ability to do things quicker, easier, and with less mess. And although technology has its drawbacks, there's no way most of us would want to go back to a simpler 1950s, where we couldn't defrost a roast in the microwave, flip open a cell phone for directions, or use a hand-held hair dryer to put lasting bounce in our style. Simply put, a life with better technology is a life that is easier—sort of.

Unfortunately, progress is never completely straightforward. With every gain, we lose a piece of a simpler, less encumbered life. With every new gadget, we become more wired and less grounded. With every new virtual link, we lose a little bit of reality. And with every secular connection, we lose a little bit of the divine. The cost of our choices usually is less sensational than the gains and a lot harder to identify. Unfortunately, without taking the time to sort out the costs from the rewards, we will never know what we are missing or where we are heading. As countercultural as it is to even consider disconnecting, unloading, powering down, or rebooting, that may be exactly what it takes to refocus our lives in a way that brings us to a deeper understanding of who we are and who we were meant to be.

3

Introduction

This book is designed to help you reboot. In computer terms, rebooting is usually required after the operating system is no longer functioning the way it's supposed to. It often is accompanied by frustrating error messages, ticked-off attempts at banging unhelpful buttons, distressed calls to a help center, or threats of throwing the whole thing out the window. No, rebooting is usually not a happy thing. However, when a reboot works, the entire operating system starts running more smoothly—the way it was designed to work. Let's face it. Sometimes, our lives could use a reboot. Sometimes, we need to spend a little time powered down, thinking about how the little, everyday choices we make are altering our values, our relationships, and, most importantly, our faith. We need to figure out how our operating system has been compromised and what we need to do to fix it.

The choices I would like to focus on have to do with all the insignificant-looking ways we use communication technology to make our lives easier and more enjoyable. As many good and noble ways as there are for these gadgets to enhance our lives, it's quite possible that they also are altering our foundational operating system. We don't usually connect things such as cell phones, iPods, video games, text messages, Twitter, and e-mails with our faith, but it's quite possible that gadgets and software specifically designed to make life more efficient and entertaining have a direct impact on the depth of our Christian experience.

In other words, a life full of purpose, abundance, and profound joy may not easily fit into a Christian life inundated with technology. After all, God can work in big, loud, and efficient ways, but often God works in small, slow, and quiet ways. When we rush by or text through experiences and relationships, it is all too possible that we will completely miss the very things that God has designed specifically to give us joy and purpose. As a result, we may find ourselves skipping along the surface of spirituality with only an occasional look into the deep-running waters of a fully committed, passionate Christian life—not exactly what God had in mind. When it comes to the way we use our technology, it's quite possible that we could do a better job of using it in ways that bring us closer to what God has designed for us. It may mean that we need to reevaluate our choices and restructure our habits. We may need to take some time to reboot.

The Hyperdrive Choice

Technology is an important topic, but I don't want to overemphasize the power it has to control us. After all, a gadget or a software package can't make us be someone we are not. When it comes down to it, our modern, high-tech lifestyle is a series of choices. From the minute we roll out of bed in the morning to the minute we lay our head on the pillow, we are faced with a series of choices of how to use our technology, how to prioritize our time, and how to treat the people around us. There's no doubt that we can be productive and efficient in a way that is also God-honoring. We can use the technology that drives our culture in a way that beautifully and creatively communicates God's love and God's hand in our lives without sacrificing important values and relationships that define our faith. But it takes work and it takes time to find the balance and the opportunities. Therefore, the first thing we need to do is to make the choice to make a choice.

I recently taught a college class on communication and technology that challenged students to become intentional about the choices they were making with their technology. One of the first things I did was require them to give up their cell phones for a week. I couldn't believe the response. I saw fire in my students' eyes—the bad kind of fire. No way could they give up their phones! Their parents might call. They couldn't talk to their friends. They would lose their connection to the world. As I thought about their concerns and how it might actually be a good thing to take a break from their parents and how they live on a residential campus with most of their closest friends no more than two minutes away, I began to realize that, regardless of the reality, they felt as though they simply didn't have a choice. To live in this culture, they had to have a cell phone. Seeking out a compromise, I then said that they could just give up sending text messages for a week. There were still some students who saw that as a non-option. No class grade was worth losing their texting ability.

As easy as it is to look at my students and shake my head at the way technology has twisted the thinking of today's teenagers, I can't go too far before I see that I'm tied into the very same ways of thinking. For instance, when I think about changing the way I use e-mail, the television, or my computer, it's a non-option. Give them up? No way! I need them. I simply don't have a choice, and it's just not worth it. After my classroom experience, I stopped to consider how my technology was shaping me. I found that, on one hand, I could be proud of the fact that I didn't spend hours at a time playing Grand Theft Auto or checking my Facebook account as my students do. On the other hand, I had to admit that I often labeled the act of watching a DVD in a dark room with my kids "quality time." I might not be able to type text messages behind my back during lectures like my students, but I could regularly be found checking e-mails at eleven o'clock at night from my dining room table.

Somewhere, and at some time, I had a choice. I had a choice about how I would use my technology to make my life better. But when that choice became critical, I didn't stop to take the time to think about the way my technology was changing me. And as the technology became more integrated into the way I live, it moved from being a fun gadget to an absolute essential. Technology has a way of changing our lives in small increments, each one overshadowing the choice we may have had to go back to how it was before.

Integrated and Intentional Hyperdrive

In so many ways, technology is changing us. It subtly takes away our choices, and it changes what we value most. Here's a challenge for you to think about as you begin reading this book: Do you have control over the way you use technology? Do you see how your choice of communicating with others may be drawing you closer or taking you further from the excitement and focus of living out your calling? Is it possible that God has got something far more exhilarating for you than what our culture has to offer through virtual relationships and high-speed connections? Have you been paying attention to the choices you make?

It is my hope that this book will help you begin the process of identifying how you are using technology. I will explore three areas where I see how our unexamined choices regarding technology may unintentionally be altering our fundamental operating system. They include our values, relationships, and the way we view our Creator. While I believe that it is important to examine negative ways in which technology may be impacting us, my ultimate goal is to help you use technology well. I would like to inspire you to creatively and intentionally balance high-tech benefits with the demands of a decidedly no-tech God. Hopefully, it will get you brainstorming about new ways to experience the Christian life with or without high-tech gadgetry. Hopefully, it will help you figure out how to reboot your current habits and refresh your fundamental commitments. At the very least, I hope that it will motivate you to stop and think.

Shift

1. Make a list of the pieces of technology that you use the most.
2. For each technology listed, consider why you started using it in the first place. Has its role changed since you started using it? If you wanted to give it up, could you?
3. For each piece of technology, list one thing that you "lose" when you choose to use it. Then brainstorm one or two ways you could readjust things to turn that loss into a gain.

Esc

Spend some time right now praying over your use of technology. Go through each thing on your list and quietly pray that God would open your heart and tune in your mind to how that gadget or website might be changing you. Then, one by one, give control over that piece of technology to God.

Part 1

Values

According to Wiktionary (a wiki-based online dictionary), *values* can be defined as something "one deems to be correct and desirable in life, especially regarding personal conduct."[1] It's no surprise that what is valued in culture today is very different from what was valued two hundred years ago. For example, at the turn of the century, things such as lifelong relationships, high-quality workmanship, and restrained behavior were considered good and healthy. People worked for the same company all of their lives and kept close to the same family and friends year after year. When something was made, whether a quilt or a house, speed and efficiency of production were not as important as the quality of the product itself. People expected certain things and judged individuals based on how well these values were displayed.

Although we certainly still value these kinds of qualities in today's culture, they often take a back seat to other values such as individuality, change, and efficiency. As we look at how technology is shifting our way of thinking, it's helpful to begin with a broad view of our cultural values. As technology allows us to do more things, faster and easier, we may find that our values are slowly changing to incorporate the advantages provided by our high-tech gadgets. However, these changes may require sacrificing important values that are too important to neglect.

In an effort to conform our use of technology to better reflect our faith, it's important to look at how technology slowly transforms what we see as "correct and desirable in life." The three value shifts I would like to explore involve the way we define reality, the speed at which we live life, and the manner in which we fill our minds.

Ctrl+Alt+Del

Is the following section for you? If you can answer yes to any of these questions, you had better keep reading.

1. Was the last time there was silence in your house the last day the power went out?
2. Do you feel closer to Ryan Seacrest and Jack Bauer than you do to your teenager?
3. Do you get ticked off that Minute Rice takes longer than a minute to cook?
4. Do you have trouble understanding why the commute to work in the morning with the radio blaring, the cell phone ringing, the child complaining, and the coffee balancing seems so very long?
5. Is the only quiet time you have accompanied by snoring?
6. Would you rather keep working on a computer that does peculiar things than reach down and press the reboot button?
7. Are you too overloaded to read a book on the overloaded lifestyle?

Chapter 1

The Alias Factor
Remote-Controlled Adventure

Television has proved that people will look at anything rather than each other.—Ann Landers[1]

It was a long hallway lined with dark shadows and locked doors. I knew I had to get out with the secret documents. I hear footsteps behind me. Trying to block out the memory of my very handsome boyfriend, I remove the ceiling tile and jump into the hallway already in full stride. As I run, the music surrounding me intensifies. The highly toned muscles in my arms and legs begin to ache, but I know I have to get out. The door at the end of the hallway flies open as my father appears. I have but one question: Is he here to help me or to capture me?

At that moment, my fourteen-year-old plops down next to me on the couch and asks if she can stay overnight at her friend's house. Out of breath, I turn to her and exclaim, "Can't you wait until the commercial!"

As much as I hate to admit it, I used to love the show *Alias*. I know it was hokey and the whole father/spy/mutant friend thing got a little complicated, but the way Jennifer Garner would run away from the bad guys—wow! The thing was, I didn't just watch her run—I *was* her. I felt the adrenaline surge. I felt my arms pump and my emotions spark. I wasn't just a slightly overweight, middle-aged mom any more. I was speedy and stealthy and gorgeous. I never moved from my spot on the couch, but I lived an exciting life—at least for one hour every Tuesday night.

And if I am completely honest, an old, cancelled spy show isn't the only time life on the screen becomes more captivating than life on the couch. Whether it's a movie filled with exciting transforming robots, a TV drama about loss and love, or a video game with armored assassins and speeding race cars, technology serves us up a flavorful smorgasbord of emotions. These emotions feel good, they are easy to access, and we never have to move out of our comfy couch space. As technology becomes more sophisticated, it does a better job of imitating and enhancing what used to be found exclusively in real-life experiences.

An important value that has been quietly impacted by technology has to do with the worth we place on real-life experience. When movie dramas take us to fictitious places and text-based conversations mimic face-to-face interactions, the boundary between reality and "not quite reality" becomes increasingly blurred. The good part about this "not quite reality" is that it makes doing big things a lot easier. We can "talk" and "hang out" with more and more people at the same time we expressly avoid some of the messy interpersonal things that inevitably happen when people get together. We can also go places and "be" the kind of people that the old-fashioned kind of reality would never allow for.

The bad part about this "not quite reality" is that when we fill life with artificial emotions, virtual relationships, and synthetic experiences, we may unknowingly be exchanging a rich, deep experience of the living God for a life no more satisfying than the shimmer of a flickering computer screen. To understand others, our Creator, even our own souls, we may need to better understand what we give up when we settle for something less than a lived reality.

The Reality Complexity

The Cool Part

As our technology becomes more advanced, it increasingly mediates our experiences. Sometimes we don't even notice how our high-tech gadgets slowly replace the reality of seeing, touching, and being there with something a little different. Sometimes that difference is quite extraordinary. For example, in "real reality" we can't actually fly without the help of a plane. But, my favorite attraction at Walt Disney World takes away this quaint twenty-first-century limitation. The first time I went on Walt Disney World's ride *Soarin'*, I was convinced that I had been given wings. After waiting for hours in a long, sweaty line, we were ushered into a room with rows of seats attached to a huge machine. We buckled our seat belts, stuffed our Mickey ears in the compartment located under our seat cushions, and began to fly. Actually, the machine simply lifts the seats high into the middle of an IMAX screen, but it was one of the coolest things I had ever experienced. As we soared over California's coast, there was a cool, misty breeze blown into my face. As we glided over the orange groves, I caught a whiff of citrus and lemons. By the time we were lowered back onto the cement floor, I felt as if I had actually flown around the state of California. In reality, I never left the building.

It was one of the most peaceful, yet exhilarating seven minutes of my life. No wonder the lines for the ride stretch around the building. With a little creativity and a dash of technological magic, Disney had produced a wonderfully satisfying encounter that I could never have experienced in real life. And the cool thing is that this kind of simulated reality is not limited to amusement park rides. Whether it's pilots practice-landing virtual aircraft, surgeons finding tumors with digitally enhanced microscopes, or soldiers diffusing bombs in the dark with the aid of robots and night-vision cameras, technology allows us to enhance reality in ways that are stunning and significant.

As exciting as these uses of technologies are, however, I know that I don't have an IMAX screen in my living room that I can easily access. Thankfully, the benefits of a virtual reality are not limited to high-priced pieces of machinery. For instance, hundreds of thousands of people regularly spend time in a virtual space called *Second Life*. It is an entirely simulated world that can easily be accessed through the Internet. Places like *Second Life* allow users to create good looking and well dressed avatars who do things like go to nightclubs to meet people, go shopping and buy things, go to college and earn real-life degrees, go to church and worship together, or just hang out with a group of friends in a beautifully decorated family room, listening to music and playing games. It is a lot like real life, only digitized.

In addition, this virtual reality offers important experiences for people. After all, some people simply don't have access to these kinds of experiences in real life. They may be shy or uncomfortable around people. They may have disabilities, feel limited by their looks, or lack the funds to go places where people hang out. Or they may simply feel more comfortable in a controllable environment where things that happen in the virtual world have little impact on real life and real life has little impact on what happens in the virtual world.

It's easy to wonder, "What are these people are thinking?" but keep in mind that some individuals truly flourish in these environments. Individuals can build confidence in an online world that will ultimately help them become more confident in real life. Users can be freer to take risks and express their true thoughts and feelings in a world that is much more controllable. People from all different walks of life and parts of the globe can come together and meet people whom they would never have the opportunity to connect with in the real world.

One especially interesting aspect of virtual reality has to do with how many stories exist of couples that meet and fall in love. Take, for example, one story of two individuals who were introduced at an online party held by some mutual online friends. After online group dating for a while, they decided to go out (online), and eventually they fell in love (online). Since things went so well in *Second Life*, they decided to meet in real life. Well, love was in the real air too, and eventually they married in a small civil ceremony. The real ceremony, however, took place a week later online, where there were extravagant decorations and a party attended by hundreds of online friends who came from all over the world (the real world). There was online dancing, online gifts to help the happy couple start their online life together, and a special ceremony with a minister who had been licensed in *Second Life* to perform weddings. They went on a fantastic online honeymoon and had a memorable time. Keep in mind that they were doing all of this while each of them was sitting at a desk, typing on a different computer, located in the same small house in England.

What makes this story particularly interesting is that as time went on, they began to have real-life marital problems. She eventually filed for divorce, claiming that he had been having an online affair with someone in *Second Life*. He said that he never had online sexual relations with this online friend, so it became hard to determine if there were grounds for a divorce in real life. Eventually they parted, however, both knowing that the trust was gone. Unfortunately, their split ruined both their real-life and online lives together.

No matter the outcome of certain relationships, virtual worlds and online conversations can provide space for remarkably fulfilling and significant relationships. These relationships and interactions might look different from what we are used to, but they still involve individuals who are finding a meaningful connection.

The Questionable Part

It's no surprise that as technology advances, reality becomes harder to recognize. Avatars, virtual-reality programs, and stereophonic high-def sights and sounds slowly move us into a world that envelops our senses and moves us out of a natural world into one that is creative, controllable, and completely contrived. As cool as those new gadgets are, however, I don't spend a lot of time using my avatar to pick up guys or fly around the world. In fact, I have to admit that I haven't been able to figure out how to work *Second Life* very well. Every time I enter, I either have trouble programming my clothes to stay on or I lift off into space with no apparent "Come back!" command. But even though I don't regularly reside in these other worlds, I consistently flirt with the virtual.

For instance, I find it painful to disengage from a gripping TV show. I enjoy the high-tech sound system and the big-screen TV that allow me to turn off the lights and enter a world created by a Hollywood director. I love watching and listening as a large screen descends into my megachurch auditorium and a sermon is delivered by a pastor who is preaching in an auditorium far, far away. I can even imagine that when I'm typing on my little cell phone or chatting on my computer, I'm actually sitting and talking with a friend. But here's the deal. The person I am engaging with may be real or fictitious, and the purpose may be significant or excessive. But if the message or the person or the experience comes to me through technology, it is virtual. If I'm not in a position to see it, hear it, and touch it, it's not quite the same as real life.

When technology reshapes and reformulates what is real and what is not, it's important to think about what the value is that underlies the process of exchanging one for the other. When we gain the excitement and the convenience of experiencing things in a virtual way, what are we giving up? How does anything less than a lived reality change or cheapen our understanding of who God is and what God wants us to be? How does powerful technology create a false impression of our ability to control our world? Clearly, reality is a complicated notion. Therefore, some of the foundational questions we need to ask as we begin to evaluate our technology-saturated lives are "What is reality?" and "What does it matter?"

The Important Part

As we examine where a shifting value of reality is taking us, we need to consider where it is we are trying to go. Scripture points us to how our fundamental operating system is supposed to be working. When Jesus was asked what he thought was the most important commandment of all, he said this: "Love the Lord your God with all your heart and with all your soul and with all your mind" (Matthew 22:37). Did you catch the theme? God wants everything from us—heart, soul, mind. God calls us toward this amazing focus that requires our whole being. If this is what it takes to live an exciting Christian life, then this is what we need to expect from our technology. If a piece of technology or a virtual space can enhance our ability to love God and point everything toward God, then we should embrace it.

However, if it gets in the way of a wholehearted, fully mindful, passionate love, then we need to rethink things. With this focus in mind, it is important to examine what we gain through a mediated reality and what we sacrifice. When all is said and done, we need to be willing to make choices about when virtual reality is good enough and when real reality is what will move us closer to the Christian life to which God calls us.

Shared Reality

The Benefits

In one of my favorite movies, *You've Got Mail,* Meg Ryan makes this comment: "Isn't it funny when we say that something in life reminds us of something in a book. Shouldn't it be the other way around? Shouldn't books remind us of something in life?"[2] At some point in our culture, books and movies and television began to replace the lived reality that we shared with one another. At some point, they became rooted into our shared social consciousness.

As improbable as it may sound, when we become so busy and physically disconnected from friends and family, the experiences created by mass media and social networking can give us a way to feel like part of an ongoing community. We can safely chat about a sad experience or an unsettling drama that we watched on television with people who really understand because they experienced it too. We can laugh about the same inside joke with people from around the world because we all saw the same YouTube video. Technologies such as television and the Internet can provide a way to pull a diverse and hurried society together, creating shared meaning in a way that feels significant.

I will never forget the time when this concept became very real to me. Princess Diana had just been killed in a car accident. I watched as millions of mourners from around the world struggled with what seemed like a very intimate loss. Even though I am an intelligent woman and knew for a fact that I had never met the princess and really knew very little about her, I began to feel like I had lost a friend. The most powerful part of all was the funeral. I remember sneaking out of bed at one o'clock in the morning and switching on the TV. There I sat transfixed, in my pajamas and slippers, watching as the world came together. I knew that at that very moment people in London, Tel Aviv, Hong Kong, and Pittsburgh were watching and emotionally experiencing the same thing that I was experiencing.

Those shared experiences have only become more significant in the past few years. Imagine, for a minute, how the falling of the World Trade Towers on September 11, 2001, would have been experienced differently if we had read about it in the newspaper two days later. Because of the live news feeds that were broadcast on every TV channel and Internet site around the world, we experienced the shock, uncertainty, and horror as a nation, at the same time, as the drama unfolded before us all. We became unified as a country in a way that was impossible a century ago. As our lives slip into overdrive, these shared experiences become an important part of our cultural tapestry. Technology has the ability to bring a diverse world together in a way that allows us to understand each other better and ultimately helps us find ways to peacefully communicate with one another.

The Sacrifices

As important as these shared experiences are, there are drawbacks to relying on news feeds, YouTube videos, and Hollywood productions to create common ground. It is important to keep in mind that whether these events are based on things happening in real life or in fictional life, these experiences are mediated. There is a piece of technology that sits in between the reality and the viewer. There is someone sitting in an editing booth or behind a camera who is doing all the processing work for us. He or she is taking away the real threat of the drama or the true uncertainty of the event and is organizing what we see to fit into an easy-to-consume camera shot. These people are taking the entire reality of everything that is happening and are choosing one perspective to share. That perspective, in turn, becomes accepted as truth.

How different would such experiences be if, instead of watching Princess Diana's funeral on television or monitoring the collapse of the Word Trade Towers on my computer, my actual friend died and I went to the funeral or if I watched out my window as a horrible event unfolded right down the block? Real events experienced in real life shape us and change us. Mediated experiences buffer us from the harshest uncertainties and realities of life. Every time we sit and connect with our culture through mediated forms such as television, movies, blogs, or YouTube videos, we take a step further away from understanding the depth of the real sorrow and the height of the true excitement taking place. The connection that we build as a community becomes built less on real people and their unique struggles and visions and more on an artificially interpreted ideal.

The difference between mediated ideals and reality can be significant. If Christ is calling us to minister to our community, it would seem that we need to understand the real people and events surrounding us using more than the sound bites we receive on the evening news or the stereotypes spooned up by Hollywood producers, bloggers, and YouTubers. Caring for our world means understanding our world from the inside out. It means connecting with the real-life needs of the people whom God puts right in front of us. Shared stories can be powerful, but not as powerful as shared lives.

The Balance

If we are seeking to love the Lord our God with all of our heart, soul, and mind, we need to figure out how to balance the mediated information that we get. On the one hand, technology can create bonds that help us experience community and connection with people. That, in turn, can help us understand the fullness of God in even more exciting and significant ways. On the other hand, getting information and experiences second-hand seems to somehow limit or fragment a holistic experience that requires our body, our mind, and our soul. For instance, when we rely on mediated experiences we might miss out on opportunities to feel true uncertainty and acknowledge our real-life dependence on God. We might neglect the chance to cognitively process events for ourselves, drawing conclusions that are more in line with our fundamental operating system than what we might get from pundits or producers. We might miss the underlying truth of the story that could silently touch our soul. By letting someone else do the processing work for us, mediating the risk and uncertainty of an event, we may very well miss aspects of an experience that bring together our entire heart, soul, and mind. Technology can bring us together in a way that nothing else has in history. Overconsumption of these experiences, however, can create connections that are based on superficial, inaccurate, solitary perspectives that move us away from engaging in real-life stories and real-life people.

Stunning Reality

The Benefits

Providing significant shared experiences for a nation that feels busier and less connected is something that technology does well. Another thing that technology gives us is an appealing way to experience a little drama in our lives. And let's be honest. Who doesn't deserve a little drama? Drama is nice. Drama allows us to disengage from a tough day, to slip off our shoes and be taken away to a virtual place where we become part of an exciting or meaningful storyline. Keep in mind that this kind of disengagement is nothing new. People have been using stories to step away from reality for centuries. Whether it's Scheherazade weaving tales of Arabian nights or Charles Dickens telling a tale of two cities, stories help us feel things and experience things. So, whether we are reading a book, watching a movie, playing a video game, or having a long online chat, technology can help us experience emotions that are fun and fulfilling.

Technology often touches our emotions by appealing directly to our senses. According to cultural critic Marshall McLuhan, one of the things that technology does well is enhance one or more of our senses. For instance, a digital surround-sound system enhances our hearing, and a digital camera enhances our ability to see. Technologies such as television and the Internet enhance our ability to see, hear, and feel things that we wouldn't otherwise have access to. For instance, it is easy to experience sights and sounds from all over the world by simply scrolling through the cable TV channels. Fear, joy, and excitement are hidden in every thirty-second commercial. Love and loss are there for us to think about and ruminate on throughout the week as we wait to tune into a new episode of a favorite show.

Values

Life-and-death decisions are made in battlefields and racetracks, each situated in compelling video games and online worlds. We even find accentuated drama as we scroll through friends' and strangers' Facebook posts and online blogs. Technology invites us to pull up to a smorgasbord of senses and emotions and fill our plates.

The Sacrifices

As we use this technology to enhance our senses, however, one has to wonder how that experience trivializes our real-life senses. E. B. White acknowledged this dilemma back in 1948 when he wrote in *The New Yorker*, "Television hangs on the questionable theory that whatever happens anywhere should be sensed everywhere. If everyone is going to be able to see everything, in the long run all sights may lose whatever rarity value they once possessed, and it may well turn out that people, being able to see and hear practically everything, will be specially interested in nothing."[3] It's possible that by having the ability to experience so many things, we lose the ability to cherish the truly special things.

When I think of truly special things loosing their flavor, I can't help but think about the road trip my family embarked on last summer. Besides the motion sickness, the altitude sickness, and the sickness from listening to endless hours of mind-deadening music chosen by my husband and my teenage daughter, I had fun. What was especially interesting was our visit to Mount Rushmore. We had planned it for days. We looked at the brochures, read about the history, and watched as the signs along the freeway got bigger and came more frequently. I was psyched. As we parked the car and headed to the monument, breathing in the crisp South Dakota air, all I could think about was Alfred Hitchcock's film *North by Northwest*. I love that movie. It's the one in which Cary Grant and Eva Marie Saint are trying to evade the clutches of a foreign spy ring. As I looked around at the pine trees and the mountains, I could clearly imagine people being chased around the monument, lounging in really cool houses overlooking the cliffs or hanging from presidential eyebrows.

When we turned the corner to catch our first glimpse of the monument, I paused. It was so . . . well, little. Sure, the iconic faces were sitting there in the hillside, just like I had expected, but it was not what Alfred Hitchcock had promised me. I was a bit disappointed to learn that there were no cool houses nearby where spy rings could hang out. I walked with my family on the neatly groomed trails with safety rails that surrounded the monument. I took pictures, bought a few postcards, and even had a penny flattened in one of those machines that crunched a picture of the monument on top. But honestly, I wasn't impressed. On the car ride back home I kept asking myself, "What was my problem?" As the badlands and the open prairies flew by, I came to the conclusion that there was the small possibility that all of the TV shows I watched and the movies I loved had somehow reduced my ability to see the awe and simple wonder of nature, or at least the captivation of certain national monuments.

And nature isn't the only thing that can be overshadowed by our use of mediated entertainment. The people we hang around can become a lot less inspiring when we compare them to people who occupy space on the flickering screen or whose avatars or Facebook profiles are so confident and beautiful. Sure, we all know that these people probably aren't real, but some of them are so good-looking! Even the not so good-looking ones seem so very wise and interesting. My husband and I watched a new TV series (destined to last only one season, as it turned out) that introduced us to Robinson Crusoe. Not only was Robinson one well-built shipwrecked guy with amazing teeth, but he was also smart and courageous and, on top of that, committed to his wife. As great as my husband is, he's no Robinson Crusoe.

Now, I'm not suggesting that we explicitly or intentionally compare our spouses, kids, coworkers, or friends to people on television or in the movies. But I am suggesting that the more we become accustomed to encountering stunning people and stimulating experiences on a screen or a website, the more unimpressed we become with everything else. Just like the heroin addict needs an increasing level of the drug to feel a satisfying high, it's possible that we need more and more excitement or beauty or intrigue to become truly inspired. And where does that leave us? It's possible that when we consume large quantities of television, movies, video games, or Internet reality, we may feel like the rest of our life becomes a bit lackluster—not necessarily bad, just not stunning.

You know the bad part about living lives that aren't stunning? I don't think that humdrum lives are what God intends for us. I think that God created us to feel and experience completely stunning joy. Not the cheap stuff. Not the kind that sends a little chill up our spine when the worship band plays a rockin' riff or when the pastor makes a dramatic pause, but the kind that's deep and exciting and long-lasting. God created us with a deep desire to feel things. God created us in a way that allows us to respond emotionally to awesome examples of divine glory and love. Those experiences might come in relationships when we are completely loved by someone. They might come in nature when we are completely overwhelmed by God's creativity and majesty. Or they might come in watching circumstances fall together in ways that undeniably communicate God's faithful commitment to our lives.

Although I haven't mastered the ability to wholly and completely enjoy my Creator—the kind of joy that sparks my entire heart, soul, and mind—I'm pretty sure that I can't experience it entirely through mediated and scripted forms. I'm also pretty sure that when I thoughtlessly plug into entertainment technology, my ability to fully experience the stunning highs and the scary lows found in real life is subtly muted. When we feed our souls large doses of artificial drama, we may very well be overstimulating and underwhelming our expectations, making it that much more difficult to be moved by things that are truly spectacular. If we are searching for rich, deep Christianity, it's possible that technology may well be sabotaging the journey.

The Balance

So where does that leave us? The answer most likely lies in balance. I'm certainly not advocating a disconnection from mediated emotions. Honestly, I can't tell you how excited I get when my favorite idol goes through to the next round in a TV singing competition or my little outer-space guy finishes a level on my video game. As we consume the entertainment offered to us by our technology, however, it's important to find a balance by which can enjoy the emotions and experiences that are enhanced by our technology at the same time we point those experiences toward better understanding and enjoying God.

We can't rely solely on computer-generated emotions when the genuine thrill lies in real life. On the other hand, these mediated emotional experiences can make life more interesting. The bottom line is that God wants us to experience his divine presence with our entire heart, soul, and mind, and that includes our emotions and senses. There's no doubt that everyone needs a little drama. Technology can bring that to us in a way that's fun and relaxing. Overconsumption of this technology, however, can make our real-life drama seem a little less satisfying and a little less significant.

Big Reality

The Benefits

A third thing that technology does well is take a certain type of reality and make it even better. It becomes sort of like an "über-reality." It polishes off the messiness and pumps everything up. For example, we can go places that we couldn't even imagine before a camera brought us information and sensations from around the world. The Internet connects people who would never have had an opportunity to meet without chat rooms or blogs or websites. Online social networking sites such as Facebook allow us to keep up with tons of friends with whom we otherwise would have lost connection. We can express ourselves online in creative ways that allow people to get to know us on our terms instead of terms dictated by our culture. We have more control over how people see us and who people think we are. We can reach out to hundreds or thousands of people in the same time it takes to sit down and talk with just one. As technology increases our reach, it creates a reality that is much bigger and, in many ways, much more interesting.

There are certain implications to this kind of expanded reality. It means that I can make more connections and potentially have much more influence. Right now I have over two hundred friends on Facebook (which is nothing compared to my college students, who see anyone with *less* than two hundred friends as sort of a loser). In any one day I hardly ever talk to more than twenty or thirty people in person. However, when I posted on Facebook that it was my birthday, I had pages of people who sent me birthday greetings, each one saying nice things about me. The fact is that between blogs and tweets, Facebook messages, and YouTube videos, I can reach a huge number of people, sharing important information or just shooting the breeze about nothing special. Technology allows me to live in a world with expanded connections and increased influence.

The Sacrifices

As cool as it is to be connected to lots of potential friends, there are some drawbacks to this kind of expanded web. First of all, an expanded web means that each one of us is regularly faced with more people, more information, more ideas, more opinions, and more stuff than ever before. For instance, now that I've entered the world of Twitter, I find myself overwhelmed with tweets. Every morning I get pages of information. The challenge is that someone's tweet containing a valuable piece of wisdom from a great book will come right next to another tweet talking about someone's grocery list or their baby's bowel problems. I end up skimming through them all. Even sitting in a chat room, using instant messaging, or running a Google search can be overwhelming. In each of one of these media, lots of information comes at us pretty quickly. Unless we are keenly focused on deciphering the important underlying messages, most likely we'll miss out on the things that are most interesting and personally relevant. So, while we gain a bigger place of connection and, potentially, greater influence, we also are sacrificing the ability to distinguish what is most valuable from what is not.

The second kind of sacrifice that we make with increased connections and influence has to do with the quality of the connection.

I will discuss some of these sacrifices in greater detail in later chapters, but I should say here that there is clearly something different about a connection that occurs in real life from one that includes a piece of technology situated in between two people. Mediated communication means that we subtly alter our message to fit within the medium. As we make those alterations, we may very well be sacrificing a little bit of who we are. We may very well be sacrificing a little bit of what makes us human.

The story of Genesis addresses the beauty of unmediated communication. Before Adam and Eve decided to take a bite of the apple, they were in a perfect relationship with their Creator. They walked and talked with God in the garden, enjoying the divine presence. That's the kind of relationship we were designed for; deep, unmediated, and real. Unfortunately, when sin entered the picture, Adam and Eve could no longer talk directly with God. They could no longer bear to bask in God's presence. Instead, God chose to communicate in mediated forms. God sent prophets to deliver messages. God created written rules to help people remember what was said to them. With every prophet and every new chapter, people chose to hear what they wanted to hear, subtly changing the underlying message. They created and worshiped images that could never capture the reality of God. And as they removed themselves further from the divine presence, they behaved in ways that demonstrated that they no longer understood God's will or feared God's power.

Although our relationship with a holy and mighty God is fundamentally different from our relationship with people, the principle still applies. When we choose to replace face-to-face, real-life encounters with interactions mediated by a piece of technology, miscommunication inevitably will occur. Whether it is a small misperception of a comment or a vital misunderstanding of motive, talking with someone face-to-face provides more information and greater accuracy. Even more important, face-to-face interactions provide human presence. There is something indefinable about what it means to sit next to someone and share the same space. By being together, we share more than messages; we share worth. When we have large groups of friends and lots of different connections, we may have lots more influence, but we may also be sacrificing that intangible something that makes us who we are.

The Balance

In our culture it's easy to assume that bigger is better. Technology allows us to experience more, learn more, and connect with more people. On the other hand, we need to be careful about what a mediated reality costs us. With that in mind, we need to ask ourselves how can we fulfill the commandment to love God with our whole heart, soul, and mind in a culture that offers us so many cool ways to connect.

Let's face it. The power of technology offers huge potential. We can so easily share the love of God with lots and lots of people. We never know who might connect with the kind of faith we talk about or where that connection might take place. Whether it is through instant messaging, Facebook, blogs, or YouTube videos, God can reach the hearts of people in lots of unexpected ways. At the same time, we need to cherish our humanity. We can't be a real-life friend to all of our online buddies, but we can choose a few key relationships on which to focus. Our commitment to these individuals, as well as to our own humanity, is made most real when we take the time to spend real-life time together. Mediated reality clearly broadens the scope of our experience, but we need to make sure that those "not quite real" experiences are supplemented with the very real interactions that matter most.

Lazy Reality

When it comes down to it, there is a balance. Technology can help a fractured culture create a unified experience, provide a space to relax and enjoy a little drama, and even expand our ability to connect. On the other hand, by using these technologies in ways that are not intentional or well thought-out, our lives can also become full of artificial relationships, bland experiences and emotions, and even values that are completely at odds with what we know to be true. A final challenge facing us as we consider the role that a technology-enhanced reality should play in our lives is how to balance the good things with the many missed opportunities that pass us by every time we plop down and log in.

Choosing not to login can be a challenge. Personally, I deal with students and colleagues all day. I come home and try to be a good mom and loving wife. I feed the dog and occasionally rub her tummy. But when I have a rare evening when nothing is scheduled and I don't have to pick up or drop off a child, all I want to do is vegetate. I like to watch the stories, feel the emotions, and make the quick and easy connections.

Maybe that's one of the reasons I am so drawn to entertainment technology. The people on the screen don't demand much from me. Yes, every now and then Kathy Smith, the video workout woman, will tell me to do just a few more jumping jacks, but I know that's coming, and I can quit without her even knowing. For the most part, sitting in front of the television or behind a computer screen is a nice, safe place to be. I don't ask much of my friends, and they don't demand that I do anything but relax and think about myself.

But how does this "feed me" mindset reduce my longing for a deep Christian life? There is no doubt that Christ calls us to be involved in our world. He calls us to be salt and light. He calls us to meet the needs of the people around us. He calls us to live lives that are about more than "me," that are about something bigger, something more significant than what we experience through our entertainment and social media. We are the people he put on this earth to help him bring about peace, justice, and healing. So how does this divine and masterful calling fit with a life filled with exhaustion and a desire to just be left alone?

One of the most significant challenges with using technology is that it creates a self-centered and lazy reality. When we participate in this kind of reality, we may truly feel like we are part of something. We may feel like we are participating in the country's great political traditions and dialogue by watching the presidential debates. We may feel like we are acting as a good friend as we read through our Facebook minifeed. We may even feel like we are part of creating great cultural icons as we dial in to vote for our favorite *American Idol* contestant. We may feel like we are involved in our world when we sit and watch television and lazily log in to our computer. But let's face it. We are not.

An unintentional approach to entertainment and social technology may result in the loss of motivation. The more we tune in, the more we tune out. Slowly but surely, the needs of the people around us become less obvious, less important, less relevant. According to cultural critic and radio show host Dick Staub, "Humans sit in front of television sets, passively watching human misery unfold, while just next door, a real person faces the same problem and there is no one to help them because we're all preoccupied with our favorite characters on reality TV. When diversion becomes a way of life, we avoid the very issues to which we should be most attentive."[4]

If we are truly seeking a deep and rich Christian experience, one of the most important ways to begin is simply to look around. We don't have to look far before we can identify a colleague who needs a friend, a neighbor who needs a hand, or a family member who needs someone to listen. By intentionally seeking out opportunities to demonstrate God's real-life love, we will absolutely find them.

The first step in this process of becoming involved in our world is to change our schedules so that we have the energy to get off the couch. The second step is to power down and look around, occasionally exchanging a virtual reality for the real thing. As we seek out ways to demonstrate God's love, we become more "in tune" than we ever could using a remote control or a computer mouse. We move more in line with the unmediated, unmuted, and unimagined life that God has planned for us.

That's the beautiful thing about stepping out of our comfy couch zone. It makes us feel alive. And that feeling is something more noteworthy and more significant than the feeling we get when our

TV-show survivor outwits and outlasts or our online avatar is voted most popular. When we actually help someone and read the gratitude or the healing on his or her face, it feels good and is good. When we come alongside someone and watch as God works a miracle, we catch a glimpse of the divine, and that is something far richer and more life-changing than anything our technology can create for us. When we become part of a real community or a cause that is important, we feel good about ourselves, feel like we are making a difference. And the thing is, we truly are making a difference—a real difference.

As hyperdriven, high-tech Christians, one of the clearest challenges we face is to make sure that our technology is not removing us too far from reality. I know that when I replace real life with artificial experiences and emotions, I can't help but feel a bit malnourished and ineffective. According to Christian philosopher Jacques Ellul, when we passively integrate technology into our lives, "an imaginary mutation takes place that is continually renewed and that erases and takes the shine off reality. A screen of images is placed between me and my world—a circle of images that become so much truer than my own life I cannot rid myself of them. Television is the supremely powerful drug. I end up living my existence before the very thing that eliminates me."[5]

Reboot

Clearly, technology-enhanced reality presents a significant challenge as we begin to parse through how our foundational operating system might be compromised. In order to become intentional consumers of this technology, we need to clearly identify what it gives and what it takes away. We need to consider how the technology reduces the effectiveness, depth, and singular focus of our Christian experience. We also need to consider the tremendous potential that this technology-enhanced reality holds. Now is the time to thoughtfully consider how you might intentionally balance the good things and the bad things of a digitized reality so that your choices make sense for you. Here are a few ideas that I've come up with.

Refreshing the Connection

First of all, consider the positive aspect of how technology creates shared meaning and unifies a diverse culture. Why not use some of that shared meaning to develop real connections? For example, if you have a goal of getting more involved in the lives of the people around you, some of the shared stories from the news or movies or television might give you the starting point that you're looking for.

Here's a personal example. Last summer we visited some relatives whom I hadn't seen in over ten years. Once we arrived and unpacked, we sat around the living room and began to get caught up. The conversation was a bit strained because we didn't seem to have a whole lot in common. Sure, we got information about each other. We heard about the kids and the jobs. And it was fine. But I thought to myself, "This is going to be one long trip." Then my husband, who had been looking up something on his computer, decided to show everyone his favorite YouTube video. Everyone laughed and started sharing their favorites. (Mine happens to be the laughing baby—my new ring tone—and a video of a Japanese human Tetris game show. You'll want to look them up.) We laughed and snickered together, and even the kids came in and started popping up funny videos. That was just what we needed to jump start our visit.

Ever since then, we've shared fun videos back and forth through e-mail, cementing the bond that we established while we were there. As a result of that experience, I have also found that YouTube evenings with my kids seem to fly by as we span the generation gap in style by spending a little Youtube time together. They show me what's popular, and I show them how stupid my sense of humor really is.

YouTube is a great example of how we can use this shared reality to create bonds that may not have existed without the help of technology. Gadgets, websites, and software don't have to translate into disconnection from people. With a little creativity and energy, we can use the shared reality to provide a safe and entertaining way to connect with people who would otherwise share very little in common.

Refreshing the Emotions

The second aspect to consider when examining how technology-enhanced reality can be used well is how our emotions are stimulated. Drama and entertainment certainly can provide a wonderful way to spend an evening. Why not have that emotion or experience serve as a motivator to go out and experience something in real life?

For instance, if you are inspired by something interesting in a nature documentary, go out and take a walk. If you enjoy a movie with a sweet love story, make it a point to tell family members that you love them. Then take the time to tell them why. If you experience something exciting in a TV drama, use it as a motivator to plan an outing with your family where you seek out some new adventure. Media-created and technology-enhanced emotions don't have to be bad. If they are based in truth and are supplemented with real emotions from real relationships and real adventures, they are even better. With a little thought, we can use technology to provide the stimulation and motivation that we need to reengage in an exciting real life.

Refreshing the Relationships

If you find that you enjoy using technology to enhance your friendships, then go for it. Find ways to use the connections that you've developed to share your deep love for Christ. Find ways to cherish the people you connect with.

You might want to try a little experiment. Choose a few friends with whom you may have lost a face-to-face connection. Start paying close attention to the information you get from them, whether it's Facebook posts, blogs, tweets, e-mails, or chats. Go out of your way to respond to things they post. Pray over the things they mention. Find old pictures of when you were together and share them on Facebook. Before too long, you may find yourself drawn to giving them a call or meeting with them over coffee. When we use technology to connect with the people God puts in front of us, ultimately we'll be drawn to helping meet their real-life needs. We will be drawn to seeing them in the same way God sees us.

Values

A second idea that may help your technology assist you in meeting your goals is to intentionally talk about things that matter. Think about what God has been teaching you today. Put that on your Facebook page. Try writing a blog about something important to you. Share pictures of things that remind you of God's love. Use the influence and the opportunity that technology affords to make a difference.

Refreshing the Reality

The final aspect to consider when brainstorming ways to integrate a technology-enhanced reality is to answer the question "Why is it so hard to disengage from the screen?" One reason why the glow of the television or computer screen feels so warm is that in comparison to real life, it often appears to be a lot better. We may choose to remain disconnected from the messiness and pain of real life because real life hasn't worked out so well. Sometimes, we choose an altered reality because it's simply a lot easier and we are just plain tired. Maybe when our realities become so complex and overscheduled, it only makes sense that our default position is in front of the computer or the television. Maybe we need to consider the priorities we have that made us tired in the first place. Clearly, if we want to seek out ways to truly love God with our entire heart, soul, and mind, we need to make choices that use the power and convenience of an exciting reality without minimizing the real parts of life that God designed to give us the most joy. Technology can lull us into thinking that a mediated reality is as satisfying as real life. Our task is to parse out what part of mediated reality is helpful and what part needs to be replaced with a truly lived experience.

Shift

1. Think about the last time you really got into a movie or TV show. Describe what, specifically, made it so engaging and compelling. Was it music, lighting, camera shots, talented actors, compelling story line? Take some time to deconstruct

the experience. This may help take the artificial shine off the mediated experiences.

2. Think about how real relationships are different from relationships that we see on the screen. For instance, how is the experience of watching a movie about Jesus different from having a relationship with Jesus? List some of the things that you lose by watching the story rather than being part of an interaction.

3. Brainstorm how movies, TV shows, or YouTube videos can be used in positive ways that might enhance your Christian experience.

4. Go on a YouTube or Tangle (formerly GodTube) hunt and look for funny or inspiring videos. Then either send a link to a few friends or post it on your Facebook or Twitter page. Try to capitalize on the shared experience by also sharing something more personal or finding a real-life connection with the people you are virtually connecting with.

5. Do a production check. Go through all of the ways you express yourself online, whether it's blogs, tweets, Facebook, MySpace, or websites, and make sure that your God-centered focus is evident in everything. Think of ways you can communicate to the people you virtually connect with that you are a passionate follower of Christ.

Esc

Spend some quiet time right now connecting with the real-life reality of your Creator. Contemplate how God is made known through nature. Try writing, in your own words, some poetry like that of the psalmist—the kind that attempts to describe the glory of God. You might want to concentrate on something in nature that's really big or really small. Try using a metaphor. Don't worry, you don't have to share it with anyone, but you might be surprised. Here are a few texts to get you started: Psalms 65; 93; 97; 104.

Chapter 2

NASCAR Speed
Multitasked to the Max

If everything seems under control, you're just not going fast enough.—Mario Andretti[1]

Not everyone will agree with me, but I've found that one of the most ironic things to watch on television is a NASCAR race. It doesn't matter if you tune in on the second lap or the three-hundredth lap, it all looks the same: cars driving around a circle, over and over again. They never seem to actually get anywhere, but they sure try to get there fast. For me, if it weren't for the little moving arrows on the TV screen or the occasional explosive crash, the whole thing would seem like a huge waste of time and energy. However, I'm not sitting in the stands, feeling the rush as packs of roaring cars fly by, and I'm not strapped into the driver's seat, feeling the adrenaline pump when I pass a car at close to two hundred MPH. As Mario Andretti could tell you, there's something wonderful about speed. Speed is excitement, it's adrenaline, it's winning! And speed isn't confined to the racetrack. It's something that has become highly valued in our culture. The more high-tech our lives become, the faster we can go, the more adrenaline we can feel, and the more we can accomplish. And that's good. Right?

Well, maybe not. There was one day in particular that reminds me of what the need for speed can do to me. It was a beautiful fall day, and I, of course, was late. As on most days, I was trying to juggle too much work with my mommy taxi service, transporting children from one sporting event or concert or play rehearsal or youth group meeting to another. On this particular day I was rushing my daughter to church. We only had a few minutes, and I knew that she would have no problem chugging down a half dozen chicken nuggets by the time we hit the church's front door, so we pulled up to the drive-thru

34

and gave the girl our order. After pulling around the corner, my heart dropped. We were never going to make it. There was an endless line of cars sitting between us our and nuggets. We waited. For almost four minutes we waited. I couldn't handle it! How could this place be so disorganized? What part of *fast* food did they not understand?

As I ranted on, clutching my steering wheel, my sweet fourteen-year-old just laid back in her seat, smiling patiently at her wound-up mother. Just as I was about to lose it, the man in front of us suddenly jumped from his car and raced up to the window. He was yelling and swearing and pointing his finger at this poor little fast-food worker. As words that no fourteen-year-old should hear floated into our car, I looked at my daughter. She smiled and told me in a wise-beyond-her-years tone, "I guess some people just have a hard time waiting." I looked at her, stopped, looked at my white knuckles gripping the steering wheel, and just started laughing. I realized that she had been sitting there the whole trip, but this was the first time I truly noticed her. The two of us laughed and talked until we pulled up to the drive-thru. We kindly took our nuggets from the frazzled drive-thru girl, thanked her for her hard work and good attitude, and continued on to church.

As I drove home, I couldn't help but ask myself, "Is a chicken nugget really worth it?" Yes, technology allowed me to eat chicken-like substances in a very short amount of time, but what was I sacrificing? Maybe there's more to life than getting a happy meal in less than five minutes. Maybe there's something more important than getting around the track faster than anyone else.

Adopting a New Speed

Technology does good things for us. I truly wouldn't want to give up fast cars or drive-thru meals. But as I noted in the last chapter, when technology gives us something good, it also takes something away. With so many technical innovations, it's no surprise that speed and efficiency have become easier to achieve and more highly valued. Inevitably, as we adopt new values, we automatically end up discarding some old ones. For many of us, goals such as efficiency and productivity have gradually overshadowed things such as patience, attentiveness, thoughtfulness, and quality workmanship. Unfortunately, these undervalued characteristics are foundational habits associated with a deep and meaningful Christ-filled life.

As good as it is to be productive and efficient, I don't think that Jesus had a whole lot of good things to say about these new and improved values. When asked what was the most important commandment of all, Jesus didn't say something like "Getting as many projects done as possible" or "Being on as many committees and boards as can possibly fit in your schedule." Let me once again point to his response. He referred to the commandment "Love the Lord your God with all your heart and with all your soul and with all your mind" (Matthew 22:37). Remember, Jesus wants it all, not just the spare minutes left over in a jam-packed schedule, and not just the part of our brain we can spare when we aren't multitasking. He wants it all. And when our lives are speeding along at a velocity hyped up on technology, do we truly have the time and energy to do anything at all with our entire heart, entire soul, entire mind? As our values shift toward efficiency and productivity, do we even have the desire to do something that requires every part of our being?

This chapter examines how technology is influencing the velocity at which we live our lives, and in turn how velocity impacts the depth and quality of our existence. By looking at the choices and sacrifices that we make, we can begin to make more intentional decisions about how to push back against this characteristic of technology, and how we can slow down our thinking far enough to catch the slow and deep parts of life that are designed to give us the greatest joy and purpose.

Multitask Mania

I don't think anyone would disagree that technology has enabled us to get more done than ever before. With new gadgets and gizmos, we can multitask in ways we would never have dreamed of a few decades ago. Think of those Norman Rockwell–type scenes of an entire family gathered around a large radio, each listening intently and happily to some variety show taking place somewhere far away. When is the last time you listened to the radio without doing something else at the same time? For that matter, when was the last time your entire family, all in one place, did only one thing—anything—together?

Multitasking has taken on incredible importance since the glory days of radio and needlepoint. The slow-paced life in which people did one thing at a time and worked on it until it was done well has been replaced by a life in which we can get a whole lot more done with plenty of time left over to think of even more things to do. A major reason why we can be so productive is that new technology allows us to do multiple things at once. For instance, if I need to be driving, why not combine that with a conversation on my cell phone? If I need to be walking, why not combine that with sending some text messages? If I need to be running back and forth, grabbing files and drinking coffee, why not combine that with conversing by way of my Bluetooth earpiece? We get more done and have more conversations in ways that are both functional and stylish. But what price do we pay? Clearly, car accidents, pedestrian accidents, workplace accidents, and even spilled-coffee accidents can be attributed to our tendency toward multitasking. But it's also possible that every time we start working on more than one thing at a time, we exchange focused, quality, and thoughtful work for tasks that are only minimally completed.

From what I have seen in my own life, multitasking is my automatic fallback. I find it creeping into my work life and my home life, fundamentally changing my relationships. For instance, my cell phone allows me to talk to my child at the same time I finish grading a paper. I find that I can send a text message to my sister while listening to my husband tell me about his day. I can even keep track of a movie plot while I talk to my mother on the phone. Well, at least I think I can do all those things at once. As I get good at doing more than one thing at a time, it's very easy to streamline my relationships in a way that enhances my ultimate efficiency. Honestly, though, too often I find myself exchanging focused, meaningful human conversations for minimal interactions that completely miss much of the depth and quality of what is really being said. Richard Swenson, physician and author of the *Overload Syndrome,* puts it beautifully: "At any given moment, the most important thing in life is the person standing in front of us."[2] Unfortunately, mobile technologies such as cell phones, Bluetooth earpieces, iPods, and text messages encourage us to multitask in such a way that we completely miss out on what is taking place right in front of us. It takes us out of our physical environment, where there are real people and real events, and propels us into a place where nothing is done well.

Unfortunately, multitasked and efficiency-driven relationships often characterize our high-tech days. Lest we think that this multitask trajectory will soon slow its pace, think for a minute about what our future will look like led by today's wired teenagers. A nice, relaxing evening for my fifteen-year-old consists of music on the iPod, IM boxes blinking on and off, virtual doors creaking open and shut, Facebook profiles flashing, cell phone text messages vibrating, and a math book sitting open. It's what we used to call "homework time." But now it's more like a graceful dance that our children perform, balancing relationships, roles, and tasks in a fluid and seamless technological ballet. Our children have learned from us. They have taken our insatiable need for efficiency and busyness and turned it into an art form. Keep this in mind: the multitasking masters of today will be the managers and leaders of tomorrow.

The Benefits

Presence. When technology enhances our ability to multitask on many levels, we clearly gain some pretty impressive things. Put plainly, we gain an ability to get more things done. Seriously, I would not want to go back to the days of my Selectric typewriter and little bottles of Wite-Out correction fluid that required my undivided attention. I shudder when I think of a time long ago when I had to wait until I got home to find out what I was supposed to have picked up at the grocery store. I like being able to do things efficiently when the situation demands. I like being able to spend time with my kids or my husband even when we aren't near each other.

Let me share an example of how mediated, multitasked communication has enhanced my relationships. For three years, my husband commuted to Reno, Nevada, while the kids and I lived in Minnesota. Even though he would come back two weekends a month, he was gone a lot. Most people couldn't understand why we did it. But interestingly, our marriage was truly strengthened during that period. The reason was that we were more "present" with each other, connecting with our technology, living on opposite sides of the country than we had been living face-to-face, day in and day out, in the same house. We spent hours at night talking to each other on the phone, often while cooking dinner or watching television or lying in bed. The thing is, when you are on the phone, you actually have to talk. So we talked and laughed and shared in ways that we simply never got around to when we were in the same house together. Technology encouraged us to be more intentional about our connection. It let us experience a real sense of presence with each other. Used wisely, technology can help create a space for people to connect in intentional and significant ways.

Quality. Relationships are not the only things impacted by presence and multitasking. A second impact has to do with quality. Innovative technology clearly allows us to do excellent work. Today we can produce high-quality things on a laptop that would have required professional machinery and enormous time and energy to produce just a few years ago. Even my sixteen-year-old can put together moving and enjoyable videos, sometimes rivaling things produced by a professional movie company. Technology also allows us to multitask in ways that can be more efficient and less intrusive. And the truth is that multitasking works just as well, if not better, for certain tasks. For example, today's tech-savvy kids, by collaborating and talking via instant messages in between math or science problems, may take longer to finish their daily homework, but it's quite possible that the quality of their work is just as high as if they had done it in a quiet room with no distractions.

In fact, some of the research that I've been involved with suggests that some students become more engaged and energized to finish mundane tasks when they have occasional interruptions from fun friends and zippy technology. Multitasking can work. If none of the multiple tasks requires a great deal of cognitive space, or if we have plenty of time to deal with the cognitive lapses that occur each time we switch from one task to another, it only makes sense to multitask. Quality doesn't have to suffer, and we can remain energized and engaged while keeping busy and getting things done.

The Sacrifices

Presence. As nice as it is to have a connection whenever and wherever we want, clearly there are sacrifices we make. One of the things that we tend to lose out on is participating in the here and now, the ability to be truly in the moment. On some level we know that it's probably not good to be on the phone too often as we drive, walk, or talk our way through the real world. But what do we gain by choosing to put ourselves "in the moment"? In other words, when we finish the face-to-face conversation that we're having with a person sitting right in front of us, in spite of the fact that our cell phone is vibrating and belligerently demanding our attention, what do we benefit? I believe that we communicate something very powerful to the person we are sitting next to. We are saying, "I value you." When we walk into work or school or the grocery store and keep our Blackberry in our pocket, what do we communicate? We are saying, "I'm paying attention." Every time we choose to put away the gadget and focus on the here and now, we begin to "see" some of the important things going on around us. We might see the people standing right next to us and get the unspoken messages that they communicate. We might notice the needs of people who pass by us every day. When we multitask, using things such as cell phones to substitute a mediated reality for real life, we miss so many important things. We miss the people and the things God has put right smack in front of us.

When I think about the problem of multitasking, I can't help but consider how Jesus responded to this tension between efficiency and spending time in the moment. Of course, he had no cell phone or wireless earpiece, but he did have disciples who had schedules to keep. There were big things for Jesus to accomplish and important people for him to meet. There were crowds and questions and threats and children running around. I'm sure that sometimes it was chaotic. And what did Jesus do over and over? He noticed the people around him. For instance, when he went to get a drink of water, he noticed the woman at the well. He looked her in the eye and saw her need. He communicated worth to a woman who really needed it. What did he do when a crowd was pushing toward him, each person wanting something different? He stopped and noticed a woman who had touched his garment. He stopped walking and turned and talked with her, seeing her behavior and meeting her need. He shut out the many "urgent" tasks at hand and focused on the truly important people standing or kneeling right in front of him.

That kind of presence, that kind of awareness of what was really going on, feels so much different from what happens when we use cell phones and computers to multitask conversations with people who aren't actually there and tasks that really aren't important. When technology pulls us to disengage with the people and the world around us, that is when we need to intentionally choose to take time to be present in the here and now before we miss what was there and left.

Quality. To a certain extent multitasking is not inherently bad. What is bad, however, is when our automatic response is to slip into high-tech multitasking mode without thinking through the available choices. When we work on more than one thing at a time, whether a menial task, a conversation, or a project, we simply cannot give it as much thought and focus as we could if it were the only thing we were doing. The productivity mindset of multitasking encourages us to try to accomplish as many things as possible in a limited amount of time. It is sort of like living life on an assembly line. And let me tell you, life on an assembly line is no picnic.

Values

A few months ago, my family and I spent an afternoon at an organization called "Feed My Starving Children," a nonprofit group that packages dehydrated meals that are then sent around the world to feed hungry children. We were with a group of friends who volunteered to spend two hours packaging meals on a well-organized assembly line. I was put in charge of sealing the meal bags with a heat-sealer. As things got going, I realized that the teens on our team were fast—not just a little faster than me, but really fast. Pretty soon my "to be sealed" meal bags were piling up. They were falling over, and the rice was spilling out, and the sixteen-year-olds were hollering at me to speed it up. My life suddenly became extremely stressful. When I began my job on the line, I made sure that every bag had a straight and beautiful seal. But it wasn't long before I was just shoving those things in the sealer and slamming it shut, praying that I wouldn't seal my thumbs together. By the end, I was exhausted and amazed. We had boxes full of meals—way more than any other team. When I looked a little more closely, however, I saw bag after bag of crinkled, folded, and cockeyed seals. My husband cautioned me about any thoughts I might have about giving up my day job.

Although I don't literally work on an assembly line for a living, there are days when my job feels that way. The classes I teach, the papers I grade, and the conversations I have resemble an assembly line. They become much more about quantity than quality. I crank things out without considering the quality of the work or the worth of the conversation. Not only does this approach to work tend to exhaust and stress me, but there are also spiritual implications of valuing quantity over quality. In Colossians, the apostle Paul encourages us, "Whatever you do, work at it with all of your heart, as working for the Lord, not men. . . . It is the Lord Christ you are serving" (Colossians 3:23–24). Working with all my heart requires the kind of commitment and focus that is hard to find in a high-velocity lifestyle. On a personal level, I struggle to think of the last thing that I did that truly was of high quality—the kind of quality where I could be proud to say, "This is something I give to you, Lord." I cringe to think of the many things I do every day—good and worthy things—that I know I could do a lot better if I had a few less other things on my plate. Technology allows us to do more than ever before. Unfortunately, the tendency toward multitasking requires a certain degree of sacrifice. Every time we choose to do more than one thing at a time, we may very well be choosing to replace presence with efficiency and quality with quantity.

Manically Mismanaged Priorities

In addition to multitasking, our high-tech lifestyle also tends to be one lived fast and efficiently. Keep in mind that fast is not always bad. Although I'm notorious for overbooking my life, I do tend to get a lot of things done. I like my high-speed Internet, which gives me quick access to an unlimited amount of information, and also I like being able to use my microwave oven and George Foreman Grill to pull together a halfway decent meal for my family in just a few minutes. There's nothing wrong with speed and efficiency—that is, nothing wrong as long as the sacrifices that we make to achieve that speed and efficiency aren't costing us more than we're willing or able to pay.

Some of these sacrifices are inherent in the way our culture operates. This became quite evident to me when my daughter and I spent a month in Europe on a study-abroad trip. Among other things, I noticed an eerie difference in the way Europeans valued speed and efficiency. The first time we noticed the difference was when we went to a restaurant in Paris. We ordered off the menu, which was a little tricky because I knew only two menu items in French. (Let's just say that we had a lot of ham and cheese that month.) Then we waited. We waited *forever* for our food. As soon as we got it, we gulped it down, and then we waited for the check. We waited and waited. We looked around. Our waiter had disappeared. We sat at this little table, and as I started feeling a frustrated fidgeting set in—this trapped sensation, wondering if we were ever going to get out of there, wondering how we could see everything on our list, wondering how these Europeans failed to understand how much we had to do—I noticed something odd. I looked at the other tables. People were done eating, and they were just sitting there. They were watching other people walk by. They were looking at the sky, the river, the trees, the newsstand, and at each other. They didn't seem hurried or driven to get to the next place. They weren't busy with cell phone conversations or work on their laptop. These people, who looked like me on the outside, seemed to be running on a different internal clock. They seemed to have an ease of living and a connection with their environment, all while they nursed their cup of cappuccino. If you've been to certain parts of Europe, you know what I'm talking about. They simply take life a little more slowly and savor the richness of what they do a little more deeply.

My daughter and I decided to try it out. We spent the rest of the month encouraging each other to slow down and appreciate everything we saw. It wasn't easy, but it was invigorating. I felt my body slow down and relax. I felt my mind work at a whole new level. I began to see things and appreciate things in ways that I never would have had I figured out how to make my cell phone work there, or how to use those international calling cards, or even figured out how to GPS my itinerary and location in order to make my steps that much more efficient. In fact, it was the afternoon we got lost after trying to read a French map and ended up spending hours walking along the river, talking and dancing and making jokes about Parisian pigeons, that was the most memorable part of the entire trip. When we came back to our American culture, the velocity of life that we witnessed was almost palpable. Even at the airport I felt bustled and rushed, pushed to go faster and faster. It didn't take long before I found myself overworked, tired, late, and out of breath—just like I was before I left.

One question that I find myself asking is this: "Why do I consistently try to do so much in such a short amount of time?" I'm pretty sure that I don't get extra credit for working the most hours or doing the most "stuff." But there seems to be some small voice inside telling me that good people work hard. There are good things to be done, and so I need to do them. There are lots of people who need something from me, and it is my duty to give it to them. Quaker theologian Richard Foster describes it well: "We pant through an endless series of appointments and duties. This problem is especially acute for those who sincerely want to do what is right. With frantic fidelity we respond to all calls to service, distressingly unable to distinguish the voice of Christ from that of human manipulators. We feel bowed low with the burden of integrity."[3] Unfortunately, overworked, overstressed, overburdened Christians are not well suited to fulfill God's calling. We're important to God's work, but we aren't *that* important. According to Richard Swenson, "It is lack of faith—coupled with an inadequate view of God—to think that we have to work twenty-hour days to get everything done."[4]

I believe that one of the first steps we need to take in getting a handle on using technology wisely is to make an intentional change in our own hearts. After all, our Blackberries and e-mails can only get us going as fast as we allow them to take us. A high-velocity schedule that is propelled by guilt over not doing enough and a misplaced understanding of our own significance will never be as fulfilling as a life dedicated to the greatest commandment of all: to love the Lord our God with all our heart and all our soul and all our mind. This commandment has very little to do with productive and efficient schedules and has everything to do with a bright and singular focus. Once we take the time to establish these divine priorities, we will be much better equipped to connect with our environment. That connection will allow us to see God's priorities and God's timing. It is that connection that will ultimately make us better consumers of technology.

Ms. 120 Percent

As I ponder how to integrate technology more intentionally and wisely into my life, it's important to consider what I'm giving up when I choose to squeeze more and more things into each day. A few years ago I had the privilege of hearing a commencement address that turned out to be somewhat of an awakening for me. It was one of those things that God seemed to prepare just for me. That evening, Dr. Richard Swenson spoke to the graduating class about margins. He talked about a life that included space to breathe, space to move, space to relax, space to focus on one thing at a time, and space to respond to the things that God places in front of us. To me, his words felt like drops of water in a parched desert. That was what I wanted. It was what I needed.

One example that he gave was particularly powerful. He described the life of someone living at 120 percent and someone living at 80 percent. My first inclination was to say, "I live life to the fullest, and I'm proud of it. Call me 'Ms. 120 Percent'!" That was until I heard the implications of those lifestyle choices. He said that someone living at 80 percent, when the Little League coach is looking for volunteers, thinks, "I've been looking for ways to get to know my kids better, and I love spending time with kids. It would be a real privilege." He then said that someone living at 100 percent would respond by thinking, "I don't think that I have the time right now. Maybe next summer I could work something out." Finally, he said that the person living at 120 percent would respond by thinking something like, "Are you kidding? I hate kids! I have to go, I'm late!"[5]

Yes, Dr. Swenson was peering into my soul. I realized that my priorities had changed. I was so busy that I no longer had the time or energy to do the things that would ultimately bring me the greatest joy. I had replaced God's priorities with a cheap list of things to do. I began to see how this played out in different areas of my life. For instance, when students came into my office with questions, I saw them as interruptions, not as individuals God had placed right there in front of me with real needs and real problems. When my kids talked to me at home, all I heard was one more person wanting me to do something instead of seeing someone God had placed right in front of me to cherish and nurture. When I went to church, all I felt was one responsibility after another instead of grasping onto a unique place to experience the sabbath.

I was Ms. 120 Percent. My life certainly was productive, and certainly unfulfilling. It was that evening during that commencement address that I decided to make a change. I can't say that I've done it well, but I have learned to watch for the danger signs. When I stop seeing people and start seeing intrusions, I know that it's time to pare down my schedule and start praying for each of my students by name. When I realize that I'm no longer looking into the eyes of my children or my husband when they talk, I know that I have too much going on and I need to set aside some family time and make a real sit-down dinner. When I simply endure a sermon at church and spend the time outlining my next lesson plan or critiquing the worship band, I know that I need a break and I need to spend some time in quiet solitude and worship. When just the idea of margins and space and purpose and joy make me feel all dried up inside, I know it is time to reprioritize.

Margins

Although I can't blame technology for speeding up my life and shifting my priorities, I can identify how my gadgets and speedy connections move me toward immediate tasks and away from things that matter. Technology has a way of taking up all the down time we might have in our day, stealing the margins we used to have. For instance, if I have a few minutes between meetings, what do I do? Do I spend a few minutes reflecting on my experiences or the people I had met with during the day? Nope. That would be weird to just sit at my desk, especially when I can quickly check my e-mail, or pull up the *New York Times,* or visit my Facebook page. When I arrive at work in the morning, instead of spending some quiet time praying, thinking, or planning, what's the first thing I do? Pull up my e-mail. The problem with starting my day with these little electronic messages is that I'm immediately faced with a hundred little crises and annoying tasks that begin to fill the spaces of my day. And what about the time at home that I try to set aside as family time or relaxing time? It silently slips away each time I check my messages from home or popup the computer to do some work for just a few minutes before dinner.

As wonderful as e-mail, computers, and Internet connections are, they can slowly steal away our margins. They quietly fill up our time with things that are not all that important, tasks that are not that much of a priority, and people who aren't even there. The problem is that when these spaces are filled, when we live life right out to the margins, we lose the energy and the ability to "see" what is right in front of us and grab onto the truly great opportunities God gives us. We settle, instead, for a high-tech, high-velocity life that reshuffles our priorities and diminishes our purpose.

Time

In addition to stealing margins, technology can also redefine time. For one thing, faster technology changes our expectations of what "slow" is. Back in the letter-writing days, when people wrote in cursive script, if I responded to your letter in a week or two, that was pretty good. Back when telephones were first introduced, people sauntered over to a ringing phone. I was watching an episode of the *Andy Griffith Show* episode the other day in which someone was calling on the phone for Aunt Bea. I couldn't believe how many times that phone rang before Andy finally answered it. And the thing was, he didn't run to get it. He slowly finished what he was doing and moseyed on over to the ringing telephone on the table. I was going completely crazy watching the man! Around my house, if you don't get the phone call in the first three rings, it disappears to voice mail, where it can languish for up to ninety-nine days. "Slow" means that you grab the phone on the second ring. No dawdling here—you have to be quick in my house!

As technology advances and connections and processors are made faster and faster, undoubtedly we will feel the pull toward greater speed. That pull often comes in the expectations that we have of others—expectations to respond in a new and hurried timetable, expectations to be available 24/7. With increased mobility and efficiency, technology has contributed to a merging of office and home, work and relaxation, company time and family time. Unfortunately, what that usually means is that we often end up doing work or things associated with work for a lot more than the twenty or forty hours a week we signed up for. Many of us feel obligated to be available. We feel a guilty pull to immediately respond to the messages we get, whether it's a text message during the drive home, a phone call during dinner, or an e-mail before bed. Technology helps us to be tons more productive. If we aren't careful, however, we may end up losing the time we desperately need to slow down and regain our priorities.

As we consider how to more wisely respond to increasingly urgent demands of our time, I am once again drawn to the example of Jesus. In a number of cases, people around him demanded that he speed it up. They called on him to perform according to their urgent timetables rather than to bless according to his calm and well-ordered priorities. I can just imagine how upset Mary and Martha were as their brother Lazarus lay dying. If they had the things we have today, I'm sure it may have started with an e-mail or voice mail to update Jesus about Lazarus's condition, but their correspondence would quickly escalate into urgent text messages, pages, and phone calls. And what did Jesus do? He waited. He finished what he was doing, what was most important, and then he responded. He wasn't pushed along by his friends' opinions or demands. Instead, he was so full of his purpose and passionate about his priorities that he waited two extra days. And then recall what he did when he got to the home of Mary and Martha. He raised their brother Lazarus from the dead. That was big. That was an event that brought unexpected glory to God. Jesus clearly exemplified a life that was more about deep priorities than urgent tasks. As we consider how technology redefines the way we view time, it is important to keep this priority perspective, taking the effort to distinguish what is urgent from what is truly important.

Patience

In addition to placing greater demands on us to respond more quickly and work faster, technology has also impacted our ability to be patient. I, for one, have always struggled with patience, especially when it comes to baking. I freely admit that my children grew up on those sliced cookies that come in a refrigerated cardboard tube. I always tried to cook a few before my kids came home from school. I so wanted to feel like I was one of those focused, disciplined, June Cleaver–like moms who had it all together. So, every day, when my kids walked in the door from school, the house was filled with the smell of cookies. It was a symbol of something I wanted in my life but didn't have the time or patience to create. I suppose that the cookies didn't taste all that bad, and usually they had some recognizable bunny or Christmas tree shape in the middle, butthe fact is that when things get speeded up, over and over again we willingly trade high quality and yummy goodness for convenient and quick imitations that really aren't quite as good. Unfortunately, that doesn't apply only to slice-and-bake cookies; it also applies to the rich lessons and deep growth that come with patience.

Scripture is filled with passages that talk about the value of patience. Again in Colossians, Paul reminds us of how we are called to care for one another: "Therefore, as God's chosen people, holy and dearly loved, clothe yourselves with compassion, kindness, humility, gentleness and patience" (Colossians 3:12). To be fully clothed in these characteristics, not just barely dressed, is hard. Think about it. Compassion and kindness, even gentleness and patience, are not necessarily the things that are highlighted in a fast-food drive-thru line. These virtues are developed over time, often through inconvenient hardship. A God-centered heart is one that is focused on these deep qualities, qualities that are developed only as we patiently figure out how to love God with all of our heart, all of our soul, and all of our mind. That singular focus, that deep process, takes time to cultivate within our lives, and it takes time to communicate to the people around us.

Unfortunately, God's lessons are usually not convenient and usually not speedy; they are not the kind of lessons that can be hurriedly texted, posted, or tweeted. But they are the very lessons that can create within us an ability to patiently care for people in a way that is present and real. I know that some of the most important lessons in my life are the ones that God patiently taught me over a long period of time. Probably my most difficult but rewarding experiences came as a result of raising a beautiful but severely disabled child. Through the years, God has forced me to slow down and has built in deep character as I struggled to do the simplest tasks for my son. Going to the park, for instance, was not about throwing the kids into the minivan and taking off. It involved diapers, medications, a ceiling lift, a wheelchair, an accessible van, ramps, wheelchair tie-downs, and a Barney video. And that was before we even left the driveway. Everything in life seemed to be more complicated and time-consuming. On the flip side, however, the times we chose to pack it all up and take off will be forever cherished. Our trip to Disney World wasn't easy, but I will never forget the smile on my son's face as he watched the SpectroMagic Parade march down Main Street. His squeals and laughter touched my heart deeply. It gave me the kind of joy wrought with patience, energy, planning, humility, and hard work. But it was the kind of joy that is deeply transformative. Few would argue that the good things in life take time. Unfortunately, as we become more wired to respond quickly to our beckoning technology, we become less willing to patiently wait for the truly good things that God is creating just for us.

Reboot

Technology can't make us do things that we don't want to do. It is the technology, however, that makes it so easy to do more and do it faster than we should. The question becomes this: "How can we use technology in a way that promotes a lifestyle full of presence, quality, margins, and patience?"

Refreshing the Multitask

Let's begin with the problem of multitasking. Some multitasking is good, and some is bad. One of the first ways to take control of technology is to be mindful of which is which. If our multitasking takes us away from a conversation or a potential conversation, it's probably bad. That might mean turning down the radio in the car, letting a phone call roll to voice mail, or removing an earbud when we are with someone. It might mean being mindful of the people standing or sitting right in front of us. My own standard is that if I don't feel compelled to look someone right in the eye when he or she is talking, then I'm probably doing or thinking about something else, and I probably should quit doing one or the other.

In addition to preventing multitasking relationships, we need to think about how our multitasking removes us from the here and now. If what we are doing causes us to miss the people and experiences in front of us, it's probably bad. This might mean becoming more intentional about where and when we talk on our cell phones. For instance, think about a time when you naturally reach for your cell phone. For me, it's when I'm grocery shopping, or walking from a parking ramp, or eating lunch by myself. There's something cozy and safe about a nice, mediated conversation when I'm alone. But every now and then it's important to put away the phone and concentrate and act on what is in front of us. It might be the box of macaroni and cheese that we're about to buy, the happy checkout cashier, or the neighbor in the next aisle; it might be the pretty blossoms on the trees, or the way the snow crunches when it's really cold; it might even be noticing the coworker sitting alone at the next table, or the pleasant, crisp texture of the apple pie. Whatever the case, we need to be intentional about when and where we tune in or tune out.

A third way to be intentional about multitasking is to consider the cognitive requirement of the tasks. If we can do more than one task, where none of them require much cognitive commitment, it's probably good. If multitasking means that we're doing more than one thing where one of them requires some focused thinking, it's probably bad. This might mean that cooking and watching television at the same time is good, whereas writing a chapter about multitasking and helping a child with algebra at the same time might not be so good. It might also mean that there are times during the day when you simply have to close the door, turn down the radio, flip off the phone, minimize the e-mail, close down Facebook, take the IM offline, silence the tweets, and work on one task. It may mean scheduling focused time to do something and do it well. It might even mean scheduling more than one time to do something—once to complete it, the next to make it better. Technology shouldn't speed us up any faster than what it takes to do things with skill and attention.

Refreshing Our Priorities

Another way to become wise about the way technology manages us is to consider our time and our priorities. First of all, we need to be internally aware of our margins. If we are already scheduled to the edges, we need to say no to a few things. Take it from me, if you haven't done it recently, it is a gut-wrenching choice the first time you say no to something good, something worth doing, something you probably would enjoy. But as you see the difference that margins begin to make in your life, you'll be amazed at how much more energy you have and how much more you smile. And once those internal boundaries and external schedules are put into place, we need to make sure that technology doesn't steal them away. We need to figure out our priorities and stick with them.

One of the biggest thieves of my time seems is that sweet-looking little e-mail box. I have found that sometimes I simply have to wrestle my priorities back from the clutches of that flashing box telling me I have messages waiting. If you have succumbed to the power of the in-box, you may want to consider a few of these suggestions. For one thing, don't start the day with an in-box check; begin with the things that are most important. If you have to get an important report finished or a letter written, do that first. Maybe start the day by figuring out what's most important. Remember, you don't get any extra credit for responding to e-mails as soon as you get them. Try scheduling only two or three times during the day for e-mail checks. Other than that, try shutting off the new-message notification and give yourself the space to work more intently on things that usually matter more than the repeated five-minute-long e-mail interruptions that tend to flood our days. We need to remember what's important during the day and try to minimize the extra interruptions and margin stealers.

Another challenge to my priorities is the way I merge my work life and my home life. If I'm not careful, when I walk out the front door of my workplace, I take just about every piece of my job with me. I find that in between dinner and time with my family, I keep checking my e-mails or text messages and automatically respond back to whatever might come up. Even when I'm on vacation, I find that unnatural pull to use my technology to keep working on tasks and keep checking in. But in fact, most of the time we don't need to do that. Most workplace "emergencies" are not really emergencies at all and will wait until we get back. If we want to guard our priorities and increase our margins, we need to choose to more fully disconnect from work at the end of the day. Maybe this means that we check our e-mails only once when we're at home. Maybe it means that we don't answer our work phone once we pull into our garage. Maybe it means letting our coworkers know when we simply are not available. The benefit is that we can start to spend unencumbered, enjoyable time with our family. As we get good at setting our boundaries and training coworkers to respect them, it won't be long before we don't even feel guilty about not being available 24/7. All it takes is grabbing hold and taking control of the things that tend to shift around our priorities.

Refreshing Our Time

Refreshing our priorities may also mean refreshing our time expectations. For instance, if I wait more than a few seconds at a stoplight, I begin to feel like a caged animal; the wait becomes unbearable. It's at this point that I need to take a breath and get a little perspective. In light of eternity, a few seconds at a stoplight is no big deal. In fact, a fast-food meal that takes a few extra minutes in the drive-thru probably is no big deal; a sermon that goes a few minutes past noon probably is no big deal; a checkout line cashier who's a little bit slow probably is no big deal; a friend who's a few minutes late probably is no big deal; a computer that takes a few extra seconds to load a page probably is no big deal; and a coworker who takes a few extra hours to respond to an e-mail probably is no big deal. When all is said and done, the things that make us the most crazy, the things that devour our precious time, are usually no big deal.

Why is it, then, that we get so stressed waiting a few seconds here or a few minutes there? It's because technology has changed our expectations. It has reduced our response time and altered our perception of how fast things need to be done. One of the most important ways to refresh our high-velocity lifestyle is to take a "waiting reality check" every now and then. When we are feeling impatient and frustrated, we need to ask ourselves, "Is this really that big of a deal? Will waiting a little more time really hurt me in any significant way? In fact, is there some way I can cherish these few extra moments while I wait?"

Frankly, I haven't mastered waiting reality checks very well, but whenever I do catch myself getting stressed about a few extra seconds here and there, I pause to look around and reconnect with my real environment. I try to notice some piece of beauty or watch the way other people are responding around me. Probably the most important thing that these little reality checks do for me is make me aware of how I am treating the people around me, whether it's a snide little remark to the customer-service representative or a rushed "Just get in the car!" to my child. By being aware of our tendency toward speed, we can make a conscious decision to capture each waiting moment in a way that creates greater margins and more peace in our life. It's nice that technology makes things quick and easy, but we don't have to blindly adopt the high-velocity lifestyle that it offers. We can slow down enough to think about how we are acting and what is really important.

Reboot Payoff

If we aren't careful, technology can steal away precious parts of the Christian life. Whether it's a connection with our environment, quality work, focused relationships, valuable priorities, or just a peaceful way of life, we need to be intentional about how we use our gadgets to enhance the productivity of our lives. We need to give ourselves the space and the mindset whereby we can figure out how to love God with all of our heart, soul, and mind. Ultimately, when we make the decision to decelerate, there is a payoff. According to pastor Kirk Byron Jones, "It is the richer, brighter life that opens up once we slow down enough to notice more. . . . It is about having the time to taste and retaste the reality of life."[6] Doesn't that sound good? Whether it's chicken nuggets or crème brûlée, life can be tasty. We just need to take the time to make sure that technology doesn't steal that yummy flavor away.

Shift

1. Think about the last time you were forced to wait (e.g., a traffic jam, a computer delay). How did you respond? What was it that caused you to respond that way? Is there a different way you could have responded? Are there any changes you could make to help you respond more positively?
2. Which box best describes you right now?

Life at 80%	Life at 100%	Life at 120%
I have margins and peace. I see the needs around me.	I'm busy now, but surviving. I see the needs that hit me in the face.	Help! Needs! Other people's needs! I don't have time for that!

3. Is the box you picked in question 2 the place where you want to be? If not, what will it take to change things? List a couple of things you could do right away to increase your margins.

Esc

Spend some time right now reestablishing what is important to you. You may want to begin by reflecting on the commandment to love God with everything. You can find slightly different versions in Matthew 22:37; Mark 12:30; Luke 10:27. Some texts in the Old Testament present the same message: Deuteronomy 6:5; 10:12;

Joshua 22:5. Take some time to think about the differences between heart, soul, and mind. How does each one translate into a different kind of experience? Finally, take some quiet time to pray through each, recommitting your heart, soul, and mind. Stay keenly aware of things that the Holy Spirit may be convicting you of as you recommit your life to God.

Chapter 3

Earbud Captives
Amped-Over Solitude

Soon silence will have passed into legend. Man has turned his back on silence. Day after day he invents machines and devices that increase noise and distract humanity from the essence of life, contemplation, meditation.—Jean Arp[1]

One of the beautiful things about living in Minnesota is the Boundary Waters Canoe Area (BWCA), a wilderness area of some one million acres with strict limits on motorized vehicles and land use. Campers have to carry supplies and canoes in the hard way, and there are no fast-food joints, electrical outlets, or water spigots for hundreds of miles. The BWCA is a beautiful, natural place that can teach some pretty unexpected lessons. One of the most significant lessons I have learned from the BWCA is how sweet and valuable is the gift of silence. Silence is everywhere in the wilderness. When I wake up in the morning in the BWCA, I don't hear an alarm clock or the morning news or the neighbor's car. When I sit on top of a cliff and watch a beautiful sunrise, I don't hear soothing music or even an audio devotional. It is just quiet—all day and all night.

I've also learned that silence does some odd things. First, it seems to draw people toward more meaningful conversations. Because breaking the silence feels like such an intrusion, people usually take time to have something to say. There's nothing more powerful than memories made around a campfire with only the crackling of the wood, the smell of toasted marshmallows, and slow, deliberate conversation. A second thing that starts to happen is that things begin to feel more ordered. We have time to think things through and become engaged in the rhythm of nature. We become more aware of how we fit into the grand scheme of things. We think more about the here and now instead of worrying about things that might happen in the future or about what other people think about things that don't really matter. A third thing that happens is that we rely more on our senses. Instead of looking at a watch or a thermometer, we look at the sun and the clouds. Instead of reading a text message or listening to a voice mail, we look into the eyes of the person we're talking with. One of the things we gain in a life full of technology is an ability to do things with enhanced speed, greater ease, and wider influence; one of the things we sacrifice is solitude, peace, and simplicity.

As we analyze how technology reshapes us, it's important to consider the ways in which our values slowly change. We have already examined how a mediated and more exciting reality may become more highly valued than a lived and somewhat tedious reality, and how a more fast-paced and efficient lifestyle may become more highly valued than an intentional, thoughtful, and focused lifestyle. In this chapter I want to consider how technology makes our lives noisier. Sometimes, as good and helpful as technology is, we simply need to disconnect and seek simplicity and solitude. As uncomfortable and unfamiliar as those concepts might be to some of us, they don't necessarily require that we abandon all of our gadgets and connections. They do require that we make choices about when we've had enough. By looking at the benefits of solitude, I hope to motivate you to balance a high-tech life with choices that we all have about when and where we might power down.

Solitude

Let me take you back to the Boundary Waters Canoe Area. One of the first times I camped there was with a group of high school students my husband and I were working with. After hiking into the wilderness, amid the usual complaints and whining, we got to a campsite, pitched our tents, and went to bed. It was so cute. The next morning, the young women came popping out of their tents with makeup and bouncy hair. They had gotten up early to make sure they looked their best. That perky, together look didn't last long. As the week progressed, these women did a lot less popping and looked a lot less perky. They started to forgo the daily hair washing because the lakes were cold and a freezing head was no picnic. Pretty soon the makeup came off and the mirrors got put away. It was then that we all began to see an inner beauty arise. We all began to live in a way that was more simple and, ultimately, more real.

That sense of realness, of taking off the "stuff" put on us by our culture, has a certain impact. One of the things that struck me most was how the students began to be comfortable with silence. They would take quiet walks by themselves, sit on rocks and look at the lake for a long time—no iPods, no cell phones, no conversation. They would quietly paddle their canoes for hours, lost in their own thoughts as they passed by towering pines and beautiful landscapes.

When six days had passed, we packed everything up, hiked back to the van, and loaded things into the trailer. As we piled into the van, a young woman turned on the radio. Heading toward Duluth, listening to the noise coming through the speakers, we all began to feel like something had intruded into our space. The music felt like a clanging cymbal, breaking a sense of calmness that had enveloped our group during the week. That particular trip was physically hard but emotionally fulfilling and healing. There is something about silence that changes us from the inside.

A Wordy World

Think about the last time you sat in silence. Were you comfortable? Silence is so . . . well, quiet. In my house, quiet is rarely an option. My kids simply cannot read or do their homework without their music playing. If the TV isn't on, providing adequate background noise, it's the radio or phone conversations that fill the air. There's nothing worse than riding in a car when the radio doesn't work— you just have to sit there! One thing that technology has done is to add noise to our lives and to our thinking. If it isn't music, it's words. We have information, advertisements, and noise all around us. According to priest and philosopher Henri Nouwen, we live in a wordy world. "Wherever we go we are surrounded by words: softly whispered, loudly proclaimed or angrily screamed; words spoken, recited, or sung; words on records, in books, on walls, or in the sky; words in many sounds, many colors, or many forms. . . .They form the floor, the walls, and the ceiling of our existence."[2]

So, when peace and quiet is so hard to come by and feels so uncomfortable, why is it something that we should consider? How does a chapter on silence fit into the middle of a book about technology? I believe that, especially in our fast-paced, hyper-real culture, silence is simply something we can't do without. It is through solitude that we can become pointed toward the depth and the meaning that we search for in the Christian life. It enhances and enriches the way we think about things, the way we treat others, and the way God speaks to us and ministers to us. That, in turn, will help us use our technology in ways that are meaningful and consistent with our fundamental operating system.

A Model of Solitude

Pastor Gordon McDonald refers to the part of our inner being that's most impacted by a noisy culture as our "private world." It's this thoughtful, contemplative, quiet part of our soul that is refreshed through solitude. Unfortunately, when we are sucked away by busy schedules and noisy technology, we have little time or motivation to be silent. "The result is the private world is often cheated, neglected because it does not shout quite so loudly."[3] Unfortunately, when we don't take the time to care for our private worlds, we can feel disorganized, out of control, dry, and unprepared to face the challenges of the day.

Look at the example Jesus provides for us when it comes to protecting and nourishing these private spaces. Before he began his public ministry, he spent time in the desert. Sometimes I wonder why he did that. He clearly knew where the desert was, so I'm pretty sure that he wasn't lost. Certainly, he could have healed a lot of needy people in those forty days that he spent in the desert. It couldn't have been a comfortable experience out there in the hot sun. So what did he gain by removing himself from his daily schedule and the noise of the day? He gained order, perspective, focus, and strength. He knew what he needed to face the next chapter of his life. He knew that he needed time to reconnect with his Father and recommit to his purpose. "He understood what we conveniently forget: that time must be properly budgeted for the gathering of inner strength and resolve in order to compensate for one's weaknesses when spiritual warfare begins."[4] Jesus knew the value of solitude.

The Way We Think

There are a number of benefits that come from taking time to disconnect and be quiet. One of the first is that it allows us to do some good thinking. In a high-velocity lifestyle one thing that suffers is our ability to make solid, thoughtful decisions. According to Kirk Byron Jones, when we hurry through life, we tend to emphasize "fast answers over good answers."[5] Our critical thinking process often is stunted, and so "we are unable to see the larger array of options before us."[6] Decisions bathed in prayer and thoughtfulness certainly will be better decisions that reinforce our dependence on God's hand in everything we do.

In addition to helping us make better decisions, a strong private world gives us space to become better critical thinkers. We can thoughtfully put the unending stream of information, news, entertainment, and advertising into context. Richard Foster observes, "We need not merely listen to the news or read the paper, we can ponder its significance."[7] We can become more independent in our thought processes, critically analyzing the voices shouting at us. Without that reasoned thought, Gordon McDonald warns, we may become like those who are "dependent upon the thoughts and opinions of others. Rather than deal with ideas and issues, they reduce themselves to lives full of rules, regulations, and programs."[8] Thoughtfulness helps us be more purposeful in what we do and more critical in the ideas we accept.

The Way We Treat Others

In addition to shaping us into better thinkers, solitude and quiet time can transform the way we treat others. When we feel rushed, dry, and barely surviving, it's no surprise that we see the people whom God puts into our lives as interruptions. When we take the time to get refreshed and reconnected with the God of living waters, we see things in a whole different way. Henri Nouwen suggests that "solitude molds self-righteous people into gentle, caring, forgiving persons who are so deeply convinced of their own great sinfulness and so fully aware of God's even greater mercy that their life itself becomes ministry."[9] When we turn off the TV, the Blackberry, and iPod and spend time praying, reading God's Word, and meditating on what God wants for us, we can be transformed by the renewal of our mind (see Romans 12:2).

I have seen how this perspective changes things. We recently moved my severely handicapped son, Aaron, into a group home not far from our house. It was the first time in eighteen years that someone else was in charge of caring for my son, and it drove me crazy. The people who worked at the group home seemed nice enough, but I felt stressed every time I went to visit. I would walk in and immediately see that Aaron was not positioned properly in his wheelchair, or that he couldn't easily see the TV screen from where he sat. I felt like they didn't give him his feedings right, change his diapers right, or put the right clothes on him. I wondered if I could somehow set up a nanny-cam to watch them and catch them doing things wrong. Every night, when I went to bed, I worried and felt guilty.

Then my husband suggested that we begin praying, by name, for the people who cared for our son. We got a list of the people scheduled to work the next two weeks and began praying. Each morning, before checking my e-mails or reading the online paper, I earnestly prayed for Aaron, for his care, and then for each person he would come in contact with. It wasn't long before I felt God begin to melt my heart. Every time we visited the group home, I began to truly see the people working with Aaron. Instead of immediately focusing on the things they were doing wrong, I began to see God highlighting the beautiful ways they were caring for my precious son. I noticed the art projects they worked on with him, the cards they sent to my husband and me, the decorations they put in his bedroom, and the videos and toys they brought from home that they knew he would love. As I talked with the workers, I began to see how much they cared. As I better understood their personal struggles and their unique gifts, I was able to pray more specifically for them each morning. As I treated them differently, they began to open up and care for my entire family.

Over the past few months, God has changed my heart. It hasn't happened through the e-mail updates that the group home supervisor sends, or the pamphlets on transition that the hospital sends, or the websites on group homes that the county manages. It has happened through the time I have spent in quietness and prayer, releasing my hold on my son, acknowledging my dependence on my Savior, and reenvisioning the way I view the people who care for him. When people ask me how the transition is going, I can't even describe the grateful heart I have. I truly believe that a significant part of this process relates to the choice I made to take care of my private world. Big challenges require big strength and renewed perspectives. That is something we gain when we take time to disconnect from technology and reconnect with our Lord.

The Way God Speaks to Us

Put quite simply, solitude provides the space and the place where we can meet God. The apostle Paul tells us, "Do not conform any longer to the pattern of this world, but be transformed by the renewing of your mind" (Romans 12:2). For the most part, renewing of our minds doesn't take place when we watch television, listen to a worship band, text a friend, or browse the Internet. These things certainly can be helpful, but they lack a mindful, thoughtful engagement with one's own soul. Henri Nouwen sums it up well. He says that solitude is the "place of purification and transformation, the place of great struggle and the great encounter. Solitude is not simply a means to an end. Solitude is its own end. It is the place where Christ remodels us in his own image and frees us from the victimizing compulsions of the world."[10]

Reboot

Refreshing the Value

So how do solitude and technology fit together? First, we need to figure out how we can revalue silence. Silence has been slowly disappearing from our modern lifestyle. If you are unconvinced that silence is worth going out of your way to create, thoughtfully reconsider the benefits of what you might gain from an occasional disconnect. As good as some of that noise may be, we need to intentionally carve out some quiet spaces in a way that ultimately will refresh our soul.

Refreshing Solitude

Second, most of us simply need to get better at being quiet. I admit that I'm not good at it. I have trouble just sitting and thinking. When I do try to silently think and pray, it usually isn't long before I find myself quietly snoring or drooling on my pillow. True solitude and contemplation are, no doubt, disciplines that take practice and time. But this doesn't mean that I can't benefit from starting by turning down the noise.

It is all about the baby steps. It might start with getting used to silence. Maybe it means making a choice to find a quiet place in your house where you read a book or have a quiet time, or maybe it means turning off the radio on your drive to work. If the silent drive gets too long, try keeping the radio off until you hit a halfway point or until you have prayed for your coworkers or family members by name.

In addition to getting used to silence, we may need to rethink part of what we traditionally call "quiet times." There can be such a thing as "noisy quiet times," and they're great. For instance, I enjoy listening to Christian music, thinking about the words, and letting the songs wash over me. It helps relax me and focus my thinking. However, there are times when what I really need to do is to listen to the things God might have for me instead of something the singer or the DJ thought was important. There are times when I need to turn off the music, put away the daily devotionals, and spend time thinking through things and silently praying and listening. It is these times of quiet solitude that provide me the focus I need to love God with all my heart, soul, and mind. It might not happen every day, but it needs to happen.

For me, the best place to find silence, away from words, music, and people, is in nature. I strongly suggest going out for walks whenever you can. Living in Minnesota, I know all too well that walking can be a chilling proposition, but I have found that nature can communicate things about God like nothing else can. I have also found that when I walk in silence instead of with an iPod clipped on my belt, I notice the things around me. I become more in tune with my surroundings and who I am. It is easier for God's still, small voice to come through, even when I'm not expecting it.

Mother Teresa had such a profound insight into silence, especially considering the extreme amount of "noise" that must have confronted her almost every day of her life. She observed, "God is the friend of silence. See how nature—trees, flowers, grass—grow in silence; see the stars, the moon and the sun, how they move in silence. . . . The more we receive in silent prayer, the more we can give in our active life. We need silence to be able to touch souls."[11] Mother Teresa understood our need to spend time in silence, waiting for God to touch our heart, renew our mind, and strengthen our resolve. As we invest in the discipline of solitude, becoming more comfortable with silence, we can experience more of the richness that Christ promised us. Sometimes we simply need to turn down the volume so that we can turn up our connection with the divine.

Shift

Plan some time to disconnect.

1. Try implementing a regular technology sabbath. Pick one day a week when you will disconnect from something in your usual arsenal of communication technology. For instance, one of my friends refuses to start up her computer between

Saturday evening and Sunday evening. That brief break from the noise of work and world of news gives her a day to relax and more fully experience the benefits of a traditional sabbath.

2. Plan a technology fast. The discipline of fasting is one that connects us with God in truly remarkable ways. Why not use technology to create a space of sacrifice and discipline? Choose one or two pieces of technology that you feel are encroaching upon your life. Put them away for a day, a week, or a month and see what happens. Every time you think about using the technology, try instead to focus on God's call for your life. By the time you end your fast, I guarantee that you will have a much greater awareness of how the technology is impacting your life and how you can more intentionally control that impact.

Esc

Close this book, turn off any noise, and spend the next ten minutes in total silence. Then open the book and list the things that went through your mind. What is your spirit most troubled with? Which things might be insights that God was whispering to your soul?

Part 2

Relationships

As we adapt our lives to incorporate the best of our technology, we clearly have adapted our values to fit within a system of new expectations and new ways of doing things. Speed, efficiency, and progress are not bad things, but we do need to make sure that they are balanced with real-life experiences and occasional disconnections.

One theme that seems to be repeated throughout the discussion of values has to do with how technology shapes the way we treat people. Our relationships are an important part of our lives and an even more important factor in how we live out our faith. In Luke's Gospel, discussion of the greatest commandment is set in the context of Jesus' parable of the good Samaritan, which emphasizes the role of our relationships with one another. Jesus affirms that we will live if we "'Love the Lord your God with all your heart and with all your soul and with all your strength and with all your mind'; and, 'Love your neighbor as yourself'" (Luke 10:27). If we are going to truly love our neighbor this way, we need to stop and think about how technology can help us do it. We also need to determine how technology might get in the way as we try to authentically reach out to others. The following chapters look at communities and friendships, examining how they can help draw us closer to living the kind of life Christ that calls us to live.

Ctrl+Alt+Del

If you can answer yes to any of the following questions, you had better keep reading.

1. Do you ever feel lost and lonely when you are in the middle of a crowd of people and you can't get a cell phone signal?
2. Do you find it hard to listen to a family member who is blocking your view of the TV screen?

3. If you see from the caller ID that your mother wants to talk to you, but your TV show is on, do you choose the TV show?
4. The last time you felt like you were having a good conversation with your kids, did you realize that they had left the room ten minutes earlier?
5. Do you feel more connected to the baristas at Starbucks than you do with the people at church?
6. Do you have hundreds of Facebook friends but no one to call when you have nothing to do?
7. Even with all the ways you have to connect, do you still feel a little disconnected?

Chapter 4

Cotton Candy Communities
Uncommitted Obligations

Let him who cannot be alone beware of community. Let him who is not in community beware of being alone.—Dietrich Bonhoeffer[1]

The sun was shining on a beautiful North Carolina day.

"Finish your pancakes, and go outside to play," calls Aunt Bea from the living room. Opie quickly shovels in the stack and flies out the back door. With a long stick in one hand and a bunch of marbles in his pocket, Opie looks around for something to do. He skips down the sidewalk, whistling a little tune. As he passes by the barbershop, a group of men sitting in front of the shop turn and smile.

"Hey, Opie. Beautiful day!" says Floyd the barber.

"Sure is!" replies Opie as he continues on. He stops to look at the red slicker bike in the window of the toy store. Some day he's going to have enough money saved up from his allowance to buy that bike. Just like every morning, the man behind the counter notices Opie and waves.

Opie decides to drop by the sheriff's office to see if anything interesting is happening. He opens the door and greets Barney Fife, the town deputy.

"Hey, Opie," says Barney, not bothering to move his legs, which are lazily perched on the desk. Opie looks around and plops down next to Barney. Maybe he'll wait here until Aunt Bea brings lunch.

In many ways, Opie is a lucky little boy. He lives in a community where he knows almost everyone, and almost everyone knows and cares for him. He talks with old people and young people alike. He feels safe, and hanging out on a summer's day doesn't involve high-speed Internet connections or darkened rooms with big-screen TVs.

Although the town of Mayberry is a highly romanticized version of life in the 1950s, it still speaks to a version of community that is very different from what many of us experience today.

Take, for example, my neighborhood. We moved in about three years ago. We met our neighbors at a "National Night Out" event a few years ago but rarely talk to them. Don't get me wrong. We're friendly, happy neighbors. We wave every time we drive by, and I watch out my kitchen window every morning as they head off to work. I notice when they have parties or when they are out of town. But other than an occasional shared lawn-mowing pass or a misrouted postal delivery, we simply don't connect. My neighborhood isn't my community. We don't live like Opie does. We drive our kids to school in another district, we attend a church in another city, and I wouldn't trust my kids to go for a bike ride outside of our cul-de-sac.

The concept of community is much different today. I tend to find my connections not based on place, but based on shared interests. In other words, while I may not be connected to people in my neighborhood, I am strongly connected to people I work with, go to church with, and whose kids go to school with mine. The thing is, there are few if any overlaps between these groups of people. My extended family doesn't know my neighbors, my neighbors don't know my church friends, and my church friends don't know my Facebook friends—different circles, different friends, separate communities. Each one of them fulfills important needs in my life and the life of my family. Each one of them, however, looks a lot different from what I see every time I tune into reruns of the *Andy Griffith Show*. Clearly, how we define and how we experience community has changed over the past fifty years. Pastor and author Shane Hipps describes our new sense of togetherness as "cotton candy communities," where superficial commitments and artificial relationships "spoil our appetite for the kind of authentic community to which Scripture calls us."[2] This is a pretty harsh view of our transforming culture, but it's important to consider where technology is taking our communities and how that direction fits with our stated goals.

Community and Identity

Who Am I?

Think for a minute about how you see yourself. When you look in the mirror, do you notice the gray hairs and emerging wrinkles, or do you see the cheery smile? Do you see someone who is attractive or someone who is plain? Do you see someone who is valuable or someone who is just taking up space? Mirrors can be funny things. They never tell us the absolute "truth." They simply give us an image that is influenced by lots of things beyond the reflected rays of light.

Communities can act a lot like the mirrors. They tell us what we see when we ask, "Who am I?" They tell us how we fit in and what we need to do to be successful. I'll never forget my first year at college. I moved from one of the largest public high schools in the state to a small Christian liberal arts college. In high school I was plain, quiet, not terribly interesting, and I was good at playing the bass clarinet. Those were the messages I got when I compared myself to the three thousand other students I saw every day. However, when I packed up and moved to college, things changed. Actually, I don't think I changed that much, but how I saw myself certainly changed. I began hanging out with a wonderful group of women who were wise and kind but, quite honestly, not naturally outgoing.

One day, my group of friends wanted to go out for a late-night study run to a local restaurant. I was pretty tired, so I told them that I was going to stay in the dorm. I'll never forget what one friend said as she pleaded with me to come. She looked me right in the eyes and said, "You have to come. You're the life of the party!" I stopped for a second and thought about it. She was right! I really *was* the life of the party. From that moment on, I saw myself as hilarious. I was the funny one. And for the next four years I was funny and smart and valuable. I didn't play the bass clarinet so well, especially compared to this one girl who could hit the high notes without squeaking, but in comparison to the people who made up my community, I was a good public speaker and sometimes my hair really did look like Farah Fawcett's. When I look back on that time, I can see that, in reality, I didn't change all that much from high school. But the people I compared myself to did change. The messages I got from my friends and professors and coworkers helped me figure out who I was. They helped me figure out my role, my perceived value, my talents, and my weaknesses. They helped me define when I was being "good" and when I was being "bad."

That's what communities do. They help us define ourselves. Over the years, I find it interesting to think about when I have felt the most poor or stupid or naughty or plain. It all has to do with the group I was with and how I stacked up. The times when the people I hung around had lots of money, my house seemed small and pathetic. Later in life, when my friends were unemployed and didn't have much, my house struck me as spectacular. Whether it was a group of "good" people who made me feel like a rebel or "smart" people who made me feel intolerably slow, I have found that my communities become comparison groups that significantly impact how I measure what I do and what I have.

Communities also help us define our worth. Much of that worth comes in the way people interact with one another. For instance, I know that I am valued in my extended family because when I look into the eyes of my in-laws, I see acceptance. I feel valued in my department at work because when I talk with my coworkers, they genuinely listen to what I have to say. How we communicate with each other says lots about how we feel about each other. We usually don't say it in words, but we demonstrate it through our nonverbal responses—a smile, a smirk, a roll of the eyes, an interruption, or a disregard. Even when we think we are hiding what we really think about a person, it usually comes shining through. The bottom line is that, for good or for bad, our communities help shape our identities and define our worth.

Technically Formed Identities

If communities are integral in helping us form our identity, the question then becomes "How does our technology impact this important function of community?" In some ways, technology allows us to become better connected to our core communities. For instance, an e-mail listserv from our Sunday school class immediately alerts everyone to urgent prayer requests or upcoming events or issues of importance to the church. Individuals use the list to pass on recipes, insights from the Sunday school lesson, photos from a party, or an occasional funny joke or YouTube video. It's interesting because I find that I learn much more about people from these e-mails than I do on Sunday mornings. Some of the more quiet people can be very funny online. Some of them can be very sweet or very smart, but because I'm not naturally drawn to them in the ten minutes between Sunday school and church, I would never have gotten to know them had it not been for the Internet connection that we share throughout the week.

Technology allows me to get closer to people and to feel more part of a cohesive group. That, in turn, can help make the presence and influence of that group more significant. The more connected and supported I am, the more valuable I feel; the more valuable I feel, the more confident I am in assuming certain roles in the group and regarding their opinions as valid. With the help of technology, I'm able to better experience the significance of a community in my life and its influence on my identity.

Online Identities. Theoretically, the better connected we are to a community, the clearer our identity becomes. As good as technology is at nurturing these connections, however, we must keep in mind that they are fundamentally different from the connections we get by spending face-to-face time together with a core group of people. This is particularly true in communities that are created and maintained exclusively through the Internet. In places such as *Second Life* or chat rooms, people hang out, laugh, play, meet new people, and share intimate secrets in a place where their looks or real-life situations have little to do with who they are or how they act. Identity is created and nurtured in these spaces. The interesting part is that an individual's identity may have much less to do with exterior physical appearance and much more to do with interior self-perception. As a result, users may feel even more authentic online than they would with a face-to-face group of people. Many people who share in these communities swear by how closely knit and special these virtual connections can be.

As we contemplate the benefits and drawbacks of online communities, once again we are faced with the question of reality. Certainly, we can gain a sense of connection and bonding in a virtual world, but what are we sacrificing? How does an anonymous identity impact the health of a real-life identity? When a person is able to be choosy about which personal facets to reveal to others and which to conceal, he or she doesn't have to deal with the constraints that come from the physical body or from real-life family, friends, and choices. On the one hand, the ability to pick and choose the best aspects of one's identity can be liberating. People can get to know each other on a much more "real" or unencumbered level. On the other hand, identity in a virtual environment can become manufactured in a way that isn't quite consistent with a holistic sense of reality. The things that we choose to hide might be an important part of who we are. When we interact in a way that is "disembodied" or that separates our ideas from our physical being, we may be fragmenting our identity in a way that is ultimately harmful to a holistic view of who we are.

Fragmented Identities. Fragmentation certainly is a concern in a postmodern society. Even if we don't virtually hang out with a group of disembodied stranger/friends, our identities still can become splintered. For instance, we all have different stages on which we perform. I act quite differently at home with my kids dancing to the Bee Gees than I do at school being Dr. Kendall. My friends at church don't know my "zany" side very well, and my students at school don't know my "introverted" side very well. Although I am not communicating with them in an anonymous, disembodied way, I am selectively crafting my persona, sharing only certain parts of myself with each community. Some of this is a natural part of socialization, but it appears that technology has made it easier to be involved in more communities that have less and less to do with each other. So, when I'm a clown on Facebook, a serious author on my blog, a quiet lurker on the church listserv, and a frumpy, middle-aged mom sitting in my living room, and

I participate in each of these communities within minutes of each other, who am I really? If our communities help create our identity, it's quite possible that with the multiple and often competing messages we receive from each community, we develop a more fragmented, disjointed, and ultimately stressful view of who we are.

Whole Identities. Unfortunately, this hodgepodge version of who we are seems quite different from the view that God has of us. In 1 Thessalonians 5:23–24 we see that God deals with us on a holistic level: "May God himself, the God of peace, sanctify you through and through. May your whole spirit, soul, and body be kept blameless at the coming of our Lord Jesus Christ. The one who calls you is faithful and he will do it." Did you catch the healing message? God sanctifies us through and through—not just the social part, not just the private part, not just the family part, but every part, through and through. In addition, God expects us to act in a way that pulls it all together— spirit, soul, and body—each part sanctified and each part blameless. There is something about the message of wholeness that speaks life into a fragmented existence.

If we truly believe that a fulfilling and effective Christian life is predicated on the concept of wholeness and of loving "the Lord your God with all your heart and with all your soul and with all your mind" (Matthew 22:37), then we need to be cautious about the things in our life that move us toward fragmentation. Whether it's superficial involvement in multiple unrelated communities or technology that allows us to hide important aspects of ourselves, a holistic lifestyle cannot work without honesty and authenticity. This deep connection with important others is crucial to building an identity that is grounded in truth and bathed in peace. It is the kind of connection that helps us pull it all together to be kept blameless with our "whole spirit, soul, and body."

Community and Commitment

I like to think that Opie or the Griffith family never had to struggle with this modern kind of fragmentation. Most of the people they ran into each day knew them in almost every aspect of their lives. After all, it was hard to hide things in Mayberry. It's my guess that life based in a grounded neighborly community would provide a certain sense of completeness and rest. In addition to a holistic lifestyle, I bet that the Griffiths also lived a wholehearted experience. Community was everything. The people in Mayberry knew each other from cradle to grave, and they did it in a way that was heartfelt and sacrificial. As we race around with our busy schedules, hopping in the car or dialing up to one "community" after another, I'm not sure that most of us feel that deep sense of connection and oneness created and experienced by the people of Mayberry. One of the most critical functions of community is the way it draws people together and wraps itself around those people who need help, making the whole group more effective than what is experienced by a bunch of individuals.

Supportive Communities

Communities provide support. Unfortunately, even though we might see the need for a supportive community, our increasingly mobile and independent lifestyles make it much more difficult to experience the wholeness and healing that come from being physically surrounded by people who care. The places where we would have traditionally gotten support often are unavailable as we move away from family or lose touch with friends. Sure, a little Facebook note from a friend is nice, and a long call to a mom or a sister can be wonderfully healing. But if you are in desperate need of a break from the kids, a ride to work, a hand with home repairs, a broken leg, or a flat tire, Skype and text messages just don't work well. That's when a community of people who are committed to one another is needed. That's when "place" really does make a difference.

I will never forget the advice that a godly woman at my church gave me one Sunday morning as I was preparing to venture off to college. She found me in the hallway next to the sanctuary, and she leaned in closely and said, "Listen to me now. Make sure you find a good church once you get to college. You never know when you might need it." At the time, I sort of smiled and nodded, but I really didn't know what she was talking about. A few years later, however, when my second child was born with severe medical problems and disabilities, I found out for real what she meant by "needing" a church.

My son was only one month old when he experienced a cardiac arrest that wreaked havoc on his little body and our peaceful family life. During the extended periods of hospitals stays, long nights, and uncertainty that followed, I found out how truly valuable a community can be. If it wasn't for the young moms in our church who offered to babysit our five-year-old, the older ladies who made us brownies and casseroles, the retired couples who went to the hospital and just sat with our newborn, and the prayers and words of encouragement from people I didn't even know that well, I don't know how my young and fragile family would have survived.

There are times when we simply need help. We usually don't know when it will happen or where, but when we are surrounded by people who are able to physically see our needs and sacrificially step in to help, that's when community is operating at its best. Unfortunately, that kind of tangible physical support rarely happens in an exclusively virtual world situated in cyberspace or scattered among the various interest groups that we are marginally part of. It does happen, however, in churches and neighborhoods and schools where people see each other, talk to each other, and commit themselves to each other in a way that is real and present. The key is authenticity and commitment.

When we commit ourselves to a group of people and are honest about things happening in our lives, that's when communities start working. Probably one of the most effective kinds of community is one that has roots in real face-to-face encounters but also has ventured into the world of interconnectivity. These are the communities that can "see" and "feel" people's real-life needs but also are set up to use the power of technology to do something about it. Listservs, e-mail chains, and Facebook groups provide powerful ways to get things organized. They can connect people who have needs with people who can help. They can give people a place to share in a deeper way than would be comfortable or convenient in a face-to-face environment. They can provide forums for people to share and creatively brainstorm ways to meet the needs of others in their community. Giving sacrificially is what makes community such a vital part of God's design for the church. When used creatively, technology can enhance this important function.

Purposeful Communities

A second thing that communities provide is a sense of unity and purpose. I doubt that God designed us to live individual, solitary lives. As evidenced in the New Testament, communities are the mechanism through which God makes us whole. It is together that we experience real effectiveness and fulfillment. In Ephesians 4:12–13 the apostle Paul talks about God's gifts that are provided "to prepare God's people for works of service, so that the body of Christ may be built up until we all reach unity in the faith and in the knowledge of the Son of God and become mature, attaining to the whole measure of the fullness of Christ." Notice that this isn't a solitary, independent process. It's one that takes place within the context of a committed community. When God created us, God gave us certain skills so that each one of us could fulfill a different role in the body of Christ. It is by working together that we can achieve greater things and make a distinct difference in the world. It is by working together that we can be part of something bigger and better than ourselves. It is through the body of Christ that we are able to "attain the whole measure of the fullness of Christ."

Unfortunately, the busier we become and less connected we are with a physical place where people care about us and notice when we are gone, the more lonely and disconnected we can become. The less connected we are to the body of Christ, the more we sacrifice in terms of meaningful work, maturity, and "knowledge of the Son of God." The fact is that we all want to find somewhere to belong. As it says in the theme song from the TV show *Cheers,* we all want to find a place "where everybody knows your name." That's where we operate in a way that's valued and purposeful. That's where we can use the gifts God gave us in a way that fits the best and makes the biggest impact. That's where we can best understand God's purpose and calling for our life. That's where we need to make sure our technology is bringing us.

Interdependent Communities

This idea of "fit" is important. As we commit to a group, spend time together, accomplish things together, and build memories together, our lives become more and more interconnected. Unfortunately, finding a place to fit is not easy. Quentin Schultz, a communication scholar at Calvin College, identifies the challenge well: "Oddly enough, in our world of abundant messaging, we are losing both our memories and our communities. As information technology mediates the world for us, we have less direct association with others, and we consequently lose our own sense of interdependence."[3]

This beautiful sense of interdependence seems completely at odds with the way we often use our high-tech gadgets to create more independence and more mediated space between us and our friends and family. For instance, technology seems to enhance our ability to be involved in multiple communities. We have so much more choice now than we used to. We can more easily find the perfect school, church, and workplace to fit our unique set of needs. On the other hand, by flitting from one community to the next, we become less engaged and less committed to any one group. That makes coming and going, duty and disengagement easy, but long-term dedication, sticking with one another through thick and thin, and true devotion to a core community much less likely.

Communities require certain things. They need to have core individuals who are willing to stick around for the long haul. They need individuals who are willing to look for ways to sacrificially give of their time and talents to one another. They need to be honest and open. They even need to be willing to hang out with people who aren't like them and some of whom they probably aren't all that fond of. Unfortunately, these kinds of characteristics are rarely modeled or promoted in the media and are fundamentally at odds with a highly productive, highly independent, and highly technical lifestyle. As a result, we may find ourselves moving further and further away from one of the primary things that can make the Christian experience so very valuable.

A Model Community

The importance of community is nothing new. The concept of a strong Christian community floods to the forefront as we look to the New Testament experience. Jesus' disciples were deeply committed to each other's understanding and personal growth. He intentionally brought them together as a group rather than choosing to quietly mentor them as individuals. He knew that they would need each other as they ventured forward after his death. The church in Acts was a moving example of a community whose members were not only committed to one another, but also incredibly effective in fulfilling its ultimate goal.

> They devoted themselves to the apostles' teaching and to the fellowship, to the breaking of bread and to prayer. . . . Every day they continued to meet together in the temple courts. They broke bread in their homes and ate together with glad and sincere hearts, praising God and enjoying the favor of all the people. And the Lord added to their number daily those who were being saved.
> (Acts 2:42, 46–47)

What an example of a significant group that was changing its culture! How much different would this community have felt if its members had only showed up once a week for a couple of hours to sit and listen to a sermon together? How much different would this experience have been from one where this "church" group was only one of three or four groups that each person was involved with, splitting his or her time among many places and many people? How much different would this experience have been from one where, instead of meeting together every day to break bread and pray, they simply sent each other a few lines on a small piece of papyrus (an ancient text message?) a couple of times a week? Clearly, the church in Acts was different.

Now, don't overestimate my desire to fully recreate the church of Acts. I'm not quite ready to sell everything that I have and move in with people from my church (see Acts 2:44–45). I am, however, persuaded to consider how I might find ways to become more committed to fewer groups, to spend more time getting to know the people in those groups, and to make some personal sacrifices regarding choice, time, and even comfort that would ultimately benefit these groups. We simply cannot overlook or underestimate our need for community. After all, when Jesus called us to follow him, he knew that we would need some help to do it.

Reboot

Make a Choice

With these things in mind, the question is, what do we do about it? The first challenge involves the potential for identity fragmentation. When we belong to multiple, unrelated communities, none of which are based on the notion of "place" or "neighborhood," it's easy for us to feel pulled in all directions. This may sound repetitive from previous chapters, but it bears repetition: simplicity may need to take precedence over choice. In other words, we may need to search for one core community into which we can pour our time and energy. Unfortunately, this usually means reducing the number of different things that we jam into our schedules. Focus is the key. As each great opportunity for involvement pops up its lovely head, focus will help us remain intentional about sticking with fewer groups of people, choosing quality over quantity, choosing to be more deeply committed to some of the people we already know.

Make a Commitment

The second challenge with today's community involves choosing commitment. As we get swept up in a consumerist approach to life, it's easy to transfer that "use it and throw it" mentality to our communities. Easy-in and easy-out thinking points to a value system where personal choice and comfort is cherished over long-term commitment. That may be okay with cell phone plans or cable providers, but it doesn't work quite so well with relationships and communities.

This is an area in which I find myself struggling. Let me give you an example. Although my family has been involved in the same church for years, we find ourselves being pulled toward the megachurch experience. There's a newer church in my suburb where the worship is amazing and the preaching is powerful. Honestly, I like being able to drive into the huge parking lot for one of several services that best fits my schedule, walk into the sanctuary, be wowed, touched, and motivated, and then hop back into my car and be home before the Sunday afternoon football game starts. As we've made the move toward this comfortable approach to churchgoing, I feel much less pressured in regard to my schedule and my competing responsibilities. That feels good. The problem is, however, that the notion of community in a church of ten thousand is a little hard to come by. I feel less restricted but less anchored, less encumbered but less connected, more personally moved but less engaged in the meaningful work of a community.

It's my guess that as our culture goes racing along and we get more stressed, busy, and fragmented, our first response is to pull in. It's possible, however, that pulling in is exactly the response that will serve to further disconnect and disengage us. Therefore, as we intentionally focus our obligations and pare down our schedules, we need to do so in a way that keeps our commitments and engagement with a core community intact. For instance, my family has made a commitment to get involved in our new megachurch. We have had to intentionally seek out places where we fit. Ultimately, we became part of a small group. It wasn't easy, though. We had to cut out a few other things. I decided to teach fewer night classes, and my husband decided to stay in town more often. But if we want to get the full value out of our church and its community, it means making some sacrifices. In a culture that values newness, change, and choice, a strong commitment to a group of people may well move us closer to the holistic lifestyle that God called us to. This means prayerfully considering which communities are worthy of our commitment. It means intentionally considering the sacrifices we may need to make in order to follow through on those commitments.

Get Engaged

Focus and commitment are important steps to take in seeking a lifestyle that values the idea of community. A third notion to keep in mind is that of engagement. Quite honestly, this part is also difficult. Long-term commitment is a little scary. Active and holistic engagement with a group of people is also a bit daunting. Sometimes I feel that if I truly invest my time and energy into a group, I will be sacrificing my personal choices. Getting involved in the lives of others means giving up a certain amount of control—control that I work very hard to achieve. Well, maybe that's the point. If we want to feel alive, have purpose, and know God's deep and meaningful work in our lives, we may need to take the step to get truly involved in the real-life, really messy world of a community.

So, what does engagement look like? Depending on which group you have chosen to commit to, it may mean taking steps such as getting to know the other soccer moms better or organizing a morning at Starbucks with a group of friends that have drifted apart. It may mean covenanting with a group of friends to meet regularly, in person, holding each other accountable. It may mean e-mailing friends during the week, or sending tweets to someone from church in the evenings, or sharing photos of fun community events on Facebook. It may mean moving from the mediated space provided by our phones and computer connections to committing to real-life space where we can see people's needs and carry each other's burdens. The bottom line is this: it means actively searching for ways to build holistic, authentic connections with the people to whom we have chosen to commit.

Get Connected

So how does technology fit within a committed community? If we use a little creativity, technology can enhance a feeling of connection, commitment, and group identity. It can increase the influence of each group member at the same time it helps the group more effectively meet one another's needs. Here are some specific ways to get your community powered up. At the very least, you may want to consider an e-mail list. Whether it's a small group of recent roommates or a large group of parents, being able to contact everyone at once makes organizing events much easier. If you have a larger group and e-mailing sounds good, you may want to consider formalizing things a bit by creating a listserv or a bulletin board. These online applications are asynchronous forms of communication that allow members to post ideas or questions. With a bulletin board, the ideas are simply posted to a board that everyone can see and respond to. A listserv will send the post to every member's e-mail box. Both applications can be run through your organization's website or can be found for free online. Groups use these applications for asking questions, organizing things, and making requests—for example, "Does anyone have a queen-size mattress?" or "Let's put on a car wash as a fundraiser," or "Please pray for me, as Tuesday is the anniversary of my father's death." Listservs are also good for conversations. Whether it's a political topic or a theological topic, listservs allow for an interaction to take place where people can read other's thoughts and respond with some of their own. It is a great way to keep conversations going that may have started in a face-to-face meeting or event.

Some other ideas include group blogging or connected tweets. You may want to consider Friday night online chats or even developing a *Second Life* presence. If your members are on Facebook, Facebook groups might work. Unfortunately, as high-tech as Facebook groups sound, they usually are difficult to maintain. They can be good, however, to advertise for events or recruit volunteers. A final idea is to share pictures. Everyone loves pictures. They have a way of reminding people of special shared experiences. Sharing pictures can be done through Facebook or photo-sharing sites such as Flickr. Basically, when you can use technology to create a space for your group to keep in touch throughout the week and to organize things that matter, the group has an increased likelihood of creating a place that better meets the needs of the members of the community.

As important as these virtual connections are, it is important to emphasize the power of meeting face-to-face. There is simply nothing that can replace the real-live, spontaneous, uncertain, fully human experience of spending time with people who have become an important part of your life.

Get a Purpose

In an age of multiple connections and efficient relationships, we mustn't forget how important communities are in our effort to love God with all of our heart, soul, and mind. As we become more committed to fewer but more meaningful communities, we may begin to see elements of the kind of community described in Scripture start popping up. The church in Acts, a role model of cohesiveness and commitment, was incredibly effective. Its members changed one another's lives and the lives of people around them. For members of that first church, the fruit of the Spirit was more than a personal search for God-given gifts; it was a corporate functioning of the body whereby each member used his or her giftedness to help move the community as a whole. God still wants to use us in ways that are big and exciting. However, the way that God is going to get big things done in this world is probably not by using a bunch of individuals, each one guarding private space and personal rights. It's my guess that God wants to use committed groups of persons, each one willing to make personal sacrifices for the good of the whole, to achieve great and powerful things. As we search for ways to refresh our high-tech lives, let's not overlook or undervalue our central need for a core, committed and caring, community.

Shift

List the groups to which you are most committed.

1. Assess. Next to each group on the list place a number, 1–10:
   1 = I barely know the people, 10 = I know the people as well

as I know myself. Then rank the list. The first one is the community that you would like to be the most committed to, and the last is the one that is most superficial and least compelling.

2. Focus. Look at the last one or two groups. Is there some way to limit the obligations related to those groups? Is there some way to combine that group with one of the other communities?

3. Commit. Look at the highest-ranked group. Brainstorm ways you can take the initiative to increase your holistic commitment to that group.

Esc

Spend some time thinking about the fruit of the Spirit (see Galatians 5:22–23). Things such as love, joy, peace, and patience naturally spill out of someone who spends time intentionally focusing on loving God. Reflect on ways you have demonstrated (or not demonstrated) these characteristics in the presence of the community that you have chosen to focus on. As you quietly contemplate each characteristic, let God speak truth into your heart.

Chapter 5

Helicopter Friendships
Fragmented Connections

Go through your phone book, call people and ask them to drive you to the airport. The ones who will drive you are your true friends. The rest aren't bad people; they're just acquaintances.—Jay Leno[1]

When I think of friendship, one of the first pictures that flashes into my mind is that of Lucy Ricardo and Ethel Mertz from the classic 1950s sitcom *I Love Lucy*. As fun as it is to watch Lucy work on an assembly line of speeding chocolates, stuffing them into her pockets and down her dress in a losing effort to keep up, what's really fun is that her friend Ethel is right there with her. We all understand that Ethel knows better. She's the solid one who always seems to be a little wiser and a little calmer. But in every outrageous situation that Lucy finds herself in, Ethel is there to help her out. The two women need each other. Whether it's helping to take care of little Ricky, popping in for a cup of afternoon coffee, or dressing up like socialites to get big Ricky's job back, Ethel and Lucy are woven together into one story. They have the kind of lasting friendship that's hard to come by.

Their friendship stands in stark contrast to what I often find myself engaged in. I've never been terribly good at being a friend, and my high-tech life challenges my ineptitude even more. The busier I get, the harder I find it is to have that "Lucy and Ethel" kind of relationship. Because I don't seem to have time to simply hang out with my friends, I often turn to technology to help me stay connected. Whether it's a Facebook chat, a quick e-mail, a happy text message, or even a cell phone conversation squeezed into my afternoon commute, my well-connected social network somehow feels inferior to the deep bond that Lucy and Ethel seemed to share.

As we search for ways to refresh our lives, sorting through positive and negative ways to integrate our technology, one of the most prominent challenges that we face is the way technology is transforming our relationships. On the one hand, we are more socially wired and better connected than ever; on the other hand, if we aren't careful, the technology that we use to enhance our relationships may be changing them in ways that slowly remove the joy and purpose for which they were designed. By examining some of these challenges, we can be more intentional about using communication technology in ways that promote the kind of authentic relationships that we so desperately need in a world that moves further and further away from that comforting "Lucy and Ethel" story.

Hovering Friendships

The Benefits

In class one day, lecturing about relationships and social networking, I asked my students how they thought something like Facebook had changed their friendships. One young woman raised her hand and described an interesting image. She said that because of Facebook, she had more "helicopter" friends. Using the flighty metaphor, she described how she could effortlessly hover over her relationships, keeping an eye on things from a lofty level. If necessary, she could touch down every now and then to say hello, leave a wall post, or send a text. She could then quickly take off as other things came up. With the help of her helicopter, she could easily manage lots of relationships in a way that fit in well with her schedule.

This metaphor seems to effectively describe the changing face of friendships. I admit that find myself falling into the hover mode of helicopter friendships much too easily. I have enjoyed using Facebook to connect with people with whom I normally would never have time to chat. I recently connected with my best friend from kindergarten, whom I had not seen in over forty years. As it turns out, she lives just a few minutes down the highway and

89

teaches at the university I attended. We haven't actually talked, but it's nice to see pictures of her kids. I also became friends with my favorite professor from twenty-five years ago. He had a significant impact on my life, and now I know where he lives and what kind of music he likes. I'm still too nervous to send him a note, but at least I know what he's doing over spring break. Seriously, some of this stuff is so cool! Facebook has allowed me to keep up with people in a way I never would have before. In a certain sense, it reconnects me with my roots, somehow helping me feel like part of a cohesive narrative. And, honestly, there is something nice, something connected—okay, maybe something a little stalkerish—about watching other people's lives, maybe lurking in the shadows, but still feeling somehow part of their story.

Before I identify some of the drawbacks of these kinds of connections, it's important to note that the research on online social networking suggests that there are significant and long-lasting positive impacts of establishing regular connections with others, even if those connections are mediated with technology. For instance, researchers at Michigan State University found that online social networking increases many users' "social capital" and enhances existing friendships. This in turn increases self-esteem and feelings of well-being.[2] In other words, Facebook helps students to be better friends and feel better about themselves. Researchers at Pennsylvania State University also found that individuals who use IM tend to feel more socially and emotionally intimate with people with whom they share instant messages, and that their use of IM increases the desire to spend time face to face with their friends.[3] The research on computer-mediated communication seems fairly straightforward: technology can enhance and improve relationships.

My personal experience supports these findings. For instance, I have seen numerous examples of times when my kids use their technology to stay connected with friends from camp, friends who have moved away, even with friends they will see the next day. Their technology provides opportunities for relationship building that we've never had before. It really does seem to enable them to be better friends. There's no doubt that communication technology, when used wisely, can help create closer friendships.

The question, therefore, is not "Can we build true friendships using technology?" The answer to that question clearly is yes. What is not quite so clear is how technology is imperceptibly changing how we view and value our friends, especially as we experience increasing pressure to speed up and over commit. It's important to stop and consider what we gain and what we lose every time we virtually connect.

The Sacrifices

One of the clear shifts that seems to have developed as a result of things such as MySpace, Facebook, buddy lists, and networks is that the quantity of our friends or acquaintances has become something worth noting. Personally, I have over two hundred Facebook friends. Actually, I wouldn't call them "friends"; they are more like people I knew at one point but have little desire to actually talk with. I'm not suggesting that we somehow value these many virtually connected "friends" over our real, true-blue, stick-with-me-through-thick-and-thin friends. What I am suggesting is that when push comes to shove, and my schedule gets busy and I run between one community and the next, fulfilling multiple roles and obligations, I'm faced with a choice. That choice is between taking the time to truly connect, in a meaningful way, with my true-blue friends or hopping into my helicopter and efficiently hovering overhead, feeling somehow satisfied with my large, interconnected network of people who sort of like me.

In his book *The Heart's Desire,* James Houston, a scholar of spirituality, identifies this situation as living on the surface of things, where our "lives are easily described but rarely understood, busy going nowhere in particular. We live at the edges of other people's lives, too busy to listen."[4] As a result, one of the clear challenges of using technology to manage friendships is that it becomes relatively easy to swap a few quality relationships for lots of helicopter friendships.

A Friendly Example

This kind of helicopter friend seems so different from what is illustrated in Scripture. When I look at the many biblical stories of friendship, I am immediately drawn to David and Jonathan. In 1 Samuel 18–20 we hear the story of these two friends. Their story doesn't feature the same camaraderie shared by Lucy and Ethel on the assembly line of chocolates, but it does have that same bond: tested commitment that shines through. Whether it was family dysfunctions, role changes, personal doubt, or difficult spiritual challenges, God brought their two stories together because the two of them were much more effective together than either one would have been on his own. Throughout their story we see how they filled in each other's weaknesses. When one was scared, the other one talked sense. When one was unsure, the other one talked wisdom. When one was hungry, the other brought food. Although there probably were extended periods of time when they didn't see each other, sometimes hiding in a cave or lounging in the palace, wondering what was happening to their friend, I doubt that either one would have been satisfied with a helicopter friendship.

To be truly part of someone's story, like Jonathan was part of David's story, takes time and energy—time and energy that sometimes don't fit easily into our daily planners. But I guess that's the way God designed us. Ecclesiastes 4:9–10 describes it well: "Two are better than one, because they have a good return for their work: If one falls down, his friend can help him up. But pity the man who falls and has no one to help him up." When we are faced with the choice between hovering over lots of helicopter friends or diving in with a few true-blue friends—quite honestly, friends who probably will demand more of our limited resources—we need to keep in mind our design. I know that at the end of the day, I don't want to have lots of high-tech connections but find myself sitting alone with no one to help me up.

"Me" Friendships

The Benefits

A second challenge facing us as we integrate communication technology into our relationships is the gradual shift toward self-messaging. One of the nice things about current technology is the way we as consumers can also become producers. It's quite easy to share our thoughts with the world. Whether it's a personal blog, a Facebook post, a tweet, a chat room discussion, or a YouTube video, we can tell others what we think and what we feel. Technology allows us to creatively express ourselves in meaningful ways that would never exist without the Internet, cell phones, or computer programs.

The Sacrifices

As satisfying as this self-expression is, however, this approach to communication may be fundamentally flawed. One of the core elements of good communication is an ability to establish "shared meaning." In other words, there is a give and take, a two-way conversation in which one of the primary goals is to understand what the other person is trying to say. In a face-to-face conversation, that give and take might include head nods, smiles, quizzical looks, or clarifying questions. When those cues are absent, however, it becomes more difficult to make sure that the other person really gets what we are saying. We can send a text message or post a message online, be we can't be sure that the person on the receiving end truly understands. But does that really matter to us? After all, it feels kind of good just to say what what's on our mind.

Personally, I like having the ability to type through some of the things I've been thinking about. There's something nice about opening up my Facebook page and knowing that my friends want to know my "status." I can think it, feel it, and post it. With one button, all my Facebook friends can catch a glimpse of what has captured me at a particular time of day. Or maybe it's something deeper, perhaps a conflict at work or a frustration with a friend. It's so satisfying to type out every snotty thing that I've been thinking and send it all in an

93

e-mail to my sister who lives three states away. I know that she doesn't check her e-mail that often, but it feels nice to press the "send" button just the same. Whether she checks the e-mail or not, the cool thing is that as I'm typing my thoughts or feelings, I'm envisioning her responding in a caring and supportive way. In reality, she might be completely confused or entirely indifferent. In the absence of those responding cues, however, I choose to assume the things I want.

So is this kind of "interacting" really communication? Well, it feels real. In fact, scholars have pointed out that technology creates a space that encourages "hyperpersonal" communication where we disclose much deeper thoughts using technology than we would in a face-to-face context.[5] You may have felt that pull toward disclosure in a blog, a long e-mail, or even a letter. It's easy to just let it all hang out. On the one hand, this kind of self-disclosure can be healthy, helping us to process complicated thoughts in a way that is authentic and honest. It can also be an important step in deepening our relationships. On the other hand, hyperpersonal communication tends to point us not toward a relationship, but toward ourselves.

In a certain sense, technology has allowed self-disclosure to become cheap and easy. The kind of self-messaging that used to be confined to personal diaries is now being repackaged as communication, interaction, and relationship building. Whether it's deep disclosures or fun status posts, when we communicate with people we can't see and interact with people we aren't near, we have a tendency to make assumptions about how they are reacting. As a result, we de-emphasize the relationship and the other person and overemphasize our ability to say something that we think is important. If we aren't careful, we can end up replacing social interaction with soliloquy, and dialogue with a series of disconnected monologues.[6]

A Friendly "You" Example

This kind of communication seems to stand in direct opposition to the kind of communication that God designed to bring us joy and purpose. As Jesus reminded us, a focused, loving Christian walk is one in which you "love your neighbor as yourself" (Matthew 22:39).

In theory, that makes sense. Loving other people is a good thing—that's no secret. Loving the people around me as I love myself, however, seems to require a different kind of lens from the one that I would naturally use with my self-messaging Facebook posts and blog entries. It requires that I eventually move the focus from me to taking notice of what is going on in the lives of the people whom I might otherwise pass by.

Look at how Jesus describes this whole "neighborly" experience in Luke 10:25–37. He tells of a man who has been assaulted, robbed, and left for dead on the side of the road. Two upstanding religious people walk by, and each of them ignores the plight of the needy stranger. If the story was happening in our time, I could easily see one of the men walking by, chatting away on his cell phone, completely oblivious to the victim he is forced to walk around as he hurries on his way. The second man might stop long enough to tell the wounded stranger to visit his website for links to helpful resources. It is a third man, however, who fulfills the commandment to "love your neighbor as yourself." It is this man who stops what he is doing, sees the wounds and needs of the stranger, and reroutes his planned journey. It is this man who takes the focus off of his own thoughts and feelings and is perceptive enough to stop and look into the heart of someone whom God has put in his path. Whether it's a stranger in the road or a friend down the block, if we are searching for ways to refresh our tired, high-tech Christian lives, it's important that we balance our self-messaging with communication that values and seeks to really "see" the person we are talking with.

Black-and-White Friendships

A third challenge facing us as we integrate communication technology into our lives is our tendency to simplify the complexities of relationships. Oversimplification is a natural outcome of living a preprocessed, mediated life. Whether it is the news, entertainment, or relational information, when we receive information funneled through a restricted filter such as technology, we tend to miss the many complexities of what is really going on. For instance, when we are in the same room with someone, looking into the eyes of the person who is talking with us, we are offered bucket loads of information. It might be a little smirk, a sideways glance, or a slight inconsistency between what is being said and what is being communicated nonverbally. As we take in all of this rich relational information, we can appreciate the many shades of the other person's meanings, emotions, and motivations, or even his or her feelings toward us. However, when we get this relational information funneled through a keyboard, all we are left with is a bunch of text. And the thing about most text is that it is black and white. It doesn't contain the many hues and colors of what might really be going on.

Communication scholar Michael Bugeja has some tremendous insights into how highly mediated people tend to simplify their relationships. He points to the influence that things such as television have on the way we perceive and deal with others. For instance, when we absorb a lot of TV shows, we begin to understand relationships in ways that are more controllable and easier to define. The good guys and the bad guys are clearly labeled, and conflicts automatically come to a conclusion by the end of the show. It only makes sense that when we accept this kind of premise we begin to see our own experiences fitting into the same tried-and-true formulas. Eventually, when we are faced with the complexity of people who are a little good and a little bad, or with conflicts that are a little their fault and a little our fault, it's not uncommon for us to hold firm to our simplified but inaccurate perceptions.

One thing that happens when we accept these painless perceptions is that we tend to underestimate the consequences of our own actions. For instance, half-truths or comments of disrespect that we might make about someone seem less important when we can't physically see the impact that such comments might have on the lives of our friends, family, or coworkers. Let's face it. It's easier to be a little meaner, a little more uncaring, or a little more pretentious when we simply type something into a keyboard or cell phone. How different would that be if we had to say the same thing while looking our friend or coworker right in the eye? As technology moves us further away from the people we are connecting to, we become less aware of how our actions impact the people around us.

This mediated communication also makes it easier to simplify the causes of our problems. Blaming others for our misfortunes is a much simpler solution when we don't want to take the time to fully understand the complexities of the events unfolding in our lives. Unfortunately, as comforting to us as assigning blame can be, it only makes it more difficult to truly understand our own role in our problems and, ultimately, resolve the things that make our lives more stressful and irritating. As we depend more and more on technology to mediate our relationships, we may find that we are slowly trading in humility and deep understanding for quick judgments and communication that tends to be a little harsher and a little less forgiving. Bugeja says it well: "People who lack perception also lack discretion."[7] Communication technologies tend to take us one step toward misperception and one step away from understanding the true cost of our actions.

Finally, highly mediated people tend to underestimate what drives other people. Instead of taking the time to truly understand why friends and coworkers react in certain ways or make certain choices, it's much easier to make quick judgments. This probably is no surprise. As we hover around in our helicopters, relying on Facebook pages and text messages to tell us how people are doing, it becomes much more automatic to define our friends' actions as good or bad, only "guessing at motive but acting on it as though it were truth."[8] This might mean labeling someone as grouchy or uncaring without stopping to notice that in real life he or she seems unusually sad or preoccupied—face-to-face cues that would indicate that something much deeper and much more complicated is going on, cues that we don't get from an online profile or a text message. Quick and easy judgments served up to us through technology may make our lives a little easier, but clearly they make our relationships less true. As we allow technology to more fully mediate our relationships, it becomes increasingly important that we not forget the complexities that come with relationships.

Clumsy Friendships

In addition to hovering, self-centered, and simplified friendships, highly mediated relationships also move us toward somewhat clumsy friendships. We probably shouldn't be surprised by our increasing ineptitude at interpersonal communication. With every new piece of technology, we are forced to learn to do things in new ways. We learn to adapt, making the technology work for us in ways that help us meet our goals. Whether using emoticons in e-mails to clarify ambiguous messages or using words in chats to describe thoughts that normally would be expressed with a shrug or a snicker, we have learned how to communicate without the help of nonverbal cues. We have learned how to adjust our communication to work within the limitations of our new technologies. That's a good thing. The bad thing, however, is that as we gain new skills, we may be losing some of the old skills that are still necessary for building deep and enriching friendships. Many of these challenges were discussed in previous chapters in terms of changing values, but here it will be helpful to consider how these changes ultimately will impact our relationships.

Occasion

You're sitting in a meeting at work, and your cell phone rings. It's one of your kids with a question about what temperature the oven should be set at for the mid-afternoon pizza snack. Or maybe you're in a class taking in a lecture on listening and communication when you get a text message about meeting for lunch. Or maybe you want to break up with someone you are dating and decide to pull up your Facebook profile and simply change your relationship status to "single." What do all of these situations have in common? A misappropriation of something I like to call "occasion."

Occasion is something that takes into account both the message and the context. It is that holistic understanding of what is being said, how it is being said, where it is being said, and when it is being said. Each one of these elements of time and place is important as we communicate with one another. For instance, being fully committed to participating in a meeting or listening to a lecture may be of greater importance than fielding extraneous messages. Figuring out the most sensitive and appropriate way to break up with someone may be just as important as the break-up message itself. When we disregard the importance of timing or the significance of what is happening at the moment, we reduce our effectiveness as communicators. We also convey to the people we are with that our need to deal with our things is more important than remaining fully present and fully aware of what might be happening in their world. When we disregard the occasion of our interactions, we inevitably become clumsy communicators.

Consideration

A second way technology reduces our effectiveness is in the way we have slowly removed the element of thought from our interactions. In previous chapters, we noted how technology pushes us to value fast over slow, and doing over thinking. This value certainly can impact the way we communicate with others. When our technology lets us easily connect with one another, it becomes second nature to feel it and say it all in one motion—a motion that omits the thinking step. In those extra seconds we might have been able to think through things a little bit more, organizing our thoughts, considering how the message might impact the receiver.

I don't send a lot of text messages, and so I don't have too much to worry about when it comes to texting something with any kind of speed. However, I often still find myself answering e-mails in ways that completely skip the "thinking" step. I also have an annoying habit of being full of good ideas—well, at least I think that they're good ideas. In the "olden days," I had to think through how good my ideas really were before I found someone to share them with. But today, with my computer always nearby, I can just send off the next great scheme or inspiration and get the people around me all stirred up and running around. My coworkers have learned to let things settle a bit before they respond. Not everyone on my e-mail list, however, has the benefit of that shared insight. Over the past few years, I have found that when I let the good ideas or worthy responses stew a little bit more, I am better organized, waste less time, and can explain my thinking in a much more cogent fashion. I also waste less time of others who aren't forced to parse through and respond to my half-baked ideas, waiting instead for the fully cooked ones. As we adopt technology that lets us communicate in quicker and easier ways, it's important that we resist the urge to hit "send" before we have thoughtfully considered the way we have organized, phrased, and nuanced our messages. By taking those extra few seconds or even extra few days to think through things, we can become less clumsy and more intentional in our communication with others.

Empathy

A third challenge to relationships has to do with our ability to truly connect with the people who matter most. As we get caught up in multitasking and self-messaging, we might find that we are losing important interpersonal skills associated with empathy. Empathy requires the ability to "put yourself in someone else's shoes"; we identify someone's emotions and then come alongside that person and share in them. Although some people by nature are more empathetic than others, having empathy is a necessary skill in every meaningful relationship, one that distinguishes and celebrates our uniqueness and our humanity.

One of the innate skills associated with empathy is the ability to read the emotions of other people. "Reading" other people isn't easy, especially if we are preoccupied with the many stimuli that vie for our attention. It is this reading, however, that is necessary to find out what someone is really trying to communicate. Interpersonal reading skills include the ability to infer implicit, sometimes hidden meanings from conversations, sensing significance in the silences, interpreting facial expressions or pauses or posture, or translating the unspoken subtexts of the things that are said. This ability to read people takes practice and commitment. Unfortunately, as we communicate in ways that systematically eliminate these kinds of cues, we may very well be limiting the practice and skills necessary for empathy and relationship building. Ultimately, if we can't figure out what a friend is actually saying and when he or she may actually need us, we won't be able to provide the empathy and support that we want to offer.

A second skill associated with empathy is that of showing support. Some people are simply gifted at this; they see someone who is sad and come up and instinctively give them a big hug. Hugs are nice, but there are plenty of ways that don't require physical touch to come alongside someone who seems a little down or frustrated. In many ways, it just takes some good listening, the kind where we look someone in the eye and nod, smile, lean forward, and voice the occasional "hmm" or "wow." I have always felt that good listening is a beautiful gift. For instance, whenever my husband comes into the kitchen after we get home from work and asks me how my day went, I feel so cherished when he sits on the counter next to me and patiently listens to my stories or complaints. Every time he asks questions or commiserates or laughs with me, I feel that I am heard and am a part of him. I don't think that this kind of connection, this kind of empathetic bond, can be created through an e-mail response or a text message. It is this kind of communication that takes true presence and empathy. As we think about how communication technologies are changing our relationships, it's important that we resist the urge to skip over the interpersonal skills necessary for shared understanding and compassion. In our efforts to avoid clumsy communication, we need to continue to hone the skills of empathy.

Patience

A final interpersonal challenge created by our high-tech ways of communicating has to do with patience. As noted in earlier chapters, a high-tech life is one that speeds along with a vicious velocity. According to communication scholar Quentin Schultz, this high-velocity lifestyle has a direct impact on our consideration of others. "If we try to live only by the rhythms of the high-tech clock, we will lack compassion. The patient person lives not in digital time but in humane time. Patience is a means of giving time to others rather than merely claiming it for ourselves or dedicating it to instrumental pursuits."[9] Patience is the kind of rare quality that distinguishes people who are intentional about how they use their technology from those who have been swept up in the high-tech, high-speed lifestyle.

Impatient people are difficult to work with. They clumsily demand things from their coworkers, families, and friends—even the person behind the counter at Starbucks. If phone calls or text messages are not returned immediately, a tension boils deep within. If things don't go as planned, there's little room for ambiguity or uncertainty. Each interruption adds more stress. Impatient people are tightly wound and tend to regularly spring open on the people around them. Patient people, on the other hand, have disengaged themselves from the digital clock and have intentionally reengaged themselves in human time. They have built-in margins that allow them the luxury of waiting for things without much stress, connecting with people without much interruption, and enjoying things without worrying too much about efficiency and productivity.

Clearly, no one is completely patient or impatient. Much of that has to do with what's going on in our lives at any one time. Patience, however, is always a virtue. As we figure out how to avoid clumsy communication, it's important to understand the way our technology speeds up our lives and changes our expectations. It's important to regularly gauge the amount of patience that we have available to pour on the people around us.

Reboot

Whether it's a high-tech lifestyle with electronic connections and virtual relationships or a simpler lifestyle with landline phones, black-and-white TVs, and friends like Lucy and Ethel, we all need someone who cares. If we aren't careful, technology will change the ways we relate to the people who are most important to us.

Docking the Helicopter

With Jonathan and David in mind as an example of the kind of friendship for which we were designed, the first question we need to ask is "How do we disengage our tendency toward hovering high in the air and engage our willingness to put our feet on solid ground?" One of the first things that our two biblical friends did was make a commitment to one another. They told each other how much they cared. That commitment was then evident in everything that they went through, including assassination plots, secret meetings, and tearful reunions. These two friends did more than share information; they shared a bond that united their very souls.

If we want to truly invigorate our relationships, we need to make a choice to commit. We need to choose between simply reading facts on a friend's online profile and making a commitment to share our very lives. Certainly, we can't engage at a deep level with hundreds of Facebook friends, but we can pick a few people and commit to doing more than lurking. That might mean regular e-mails, phone calls, or conversations over coffee. It might mean taking the time to tell a friend how much he or she means to us. This is where technology can make our task much easier and more enjoyable. Whether it's a funny greeting card found at the copy center and mailed to an old friend, or a piece of Facebook flair that's just perfect for a daughter, or a long e-mail to a son, technology allows us to confirm our bond with our important people in lots of little ways. It also reminds us that we are part of their lives, and we had better start paying attention.

Changing the Focus

The second thing about Jonathan and David that strikes me is the way they made sacrifices for one another. Look at what Jonathan gave up to support David. He gave up his throne. That is big-time sacrifice—so much bigger than anything I have been called to sacrifice for a friend. In a culture like ours, which moves us toward self-centered relationships, we need to be very intentional about going out of our way to be there for the important people in our lives, even if it means sacrifice. And the fact is that this kind of sacrificial relationship often requires inconvenient timing that moves beyond Internet connections and scheduled events. It often requires getting up off the couch, shutting down the computer, and doing something. It requires a focus that looks beyond what's happening in one's own life and seeks out what's happening in the lives of others.

So what are the implications for a high-tech life? Maybe it means that when we read a Facebook profile that says our friend is sick, we bring over a casserole. Maybe when we read that a friend is overwhelmed and busy, we offer to babysit or run some errands. Maybe when we read that a friend has a job interview or a test, we pray and send a note. If we open our eyes, we may find that our technology has provided lots of information about what's happening with our friends. We just need to take the next step, the step that matches up the information about our friends' needs and then acts to help meet their needs.

Seeking the Truth

A final thing about the relationship between Jonathan and David that fits within this discussion has to do with the way they spoke truth into each other's lives. When Jonathan came to see David as he was hiding in a cave, David told him about the plot that Saul had devised to kill the giant-slayer and future king. Jonathan wouldn't listen. He was sure that David was mistaken. But he knew that David was committed to him, so he checked it out. Unfortunately, the plot was real. I'm sure that David did not relish the idea of telling Jonathan that his father was a murderous conniver. But David and Jonathan were committed to one another. They knew that sometimes the truth is inconvenient and messy.

The same kind of messiness exists in our relationships. Sometimes it's hard to see the role that we play in our own troubles. Sometimes it's much easier to disengage from hurt or misunderstanding and concentrate on something else. Our technology makes it so much easier to run away from problems. Because many of our relationships are mediated and virtual, it's often easier to read the caller ID and let the phone ring, leave the e-mail unopened, or delete the incoming text message. When we can't see the person whom we need to deal with, it's easy to let the conflicts remain unresolved or the difficult conversations left unspoken. On the other hand, if we want to refresh our high-tech lives in a way that renews our relationships, we need to remove the technology that stands in the way of establishing honest and true communication with those people who matter most.

With all of the new communication technologies that we've integrated into our ways of doing things, it's not surprising that our relationships have changed. When used intentionally, technology can enhance our friendships, helping us find new and even more meaningful ways to connect with one another. Our cool little gadgets can help to make us be better friends, but we must take the time to recommit to the people who are important to us, look for ways to meet their needs, and make sure that our communication is both grace-filled and honest. We need to make sure that we control our technology, not the other way around. That's when we can experience the kind of relationships that God designed us to have, the kind of relationships that give life and reveal the deep love that God wants to rain down upon us.

Shift

1. Go on a Facebook needs-hunting expedition. Scroll through some of your good friends' profiles. See if you can find the hint of a need that you can meet in a creative way. List two or three ways you can show your friends that you are paying attention and are committed to them.

2. Think of someone with whom you're upset. List ways you can use technology to help reshape that relationship. (e.g.: sending a supportive text message, composing a grace-filled e-mail, or sharing a few pictures of better days.)

Esc

Spend some time reading through the story of Jonathan and David (1 Samuel 18–20). As you read, note the things that characterized their friendship. Compare those things with the relationship that you have with one or two of your good friends. Contemplate what the biblical example of friendship might look like in a modern, high-tech culture. What things would change? What things would stay the same?

Once you are finished, spend some time quietly praying for your friends. Choose one or two whom you would like to commit to and spend some time praying about how God might use you in their lives. As you pray, think of something that you can do right now to bless them.

Part 3

Faith

Technology gives us many important things. It makes life easier, more productive, and even more social. However, as our culture promises a contemporary life of ease and speed, we need to thoughtfully contemplate how these modern gadgets also demand sacrifice. As we conclude with a discussion of ways technology will ultimately impact our faith, it will be helpful to consider how this new lifestyle has a direct impact on the most basic elements of faith. It's possible that a reprioritized and revalued faith experience will have a deep impact on how we view our Creator. Ultimately, the way we view God can change everything. After all, a God who is controllable and relegated to the same mediated reality as our other virtual experience is a God who is easily ignored. A God who defies the bounds of our technology and is the true sovereign of the universe is a God to be respected and revered.

The final chapter explores how our view of God is at the core of our view of technology. As we appreciate the full wonder of our Creator, we certainly will find an instinctive way to prioritize the many gadgets, connections, and software that fill our lives. When we love a truly awesome God with all of our heart, soul, and mind, our use of technology can't help but mirror that focus, drive, and passion. How we view God really does matter.

Ctrl+Alt+Del

If you can answer yes to one or more of these questions, you might as well finish the book.

1. If you could answer anonymously, would you say that Oprah might be just a little more powerful than God?

2. Do you feel that if you really needed to, you could describe God and what God means to you in a tweet of 140 characters or less?

3. Do you hate it when the preaching at your church gets in the way of the good music and cool videos?
4. Do you feel more comfortable watching a movie about Jesus than spending time with Jesus?
5. Does your calling have more to do with rollover minutes than with God's plan for your life?
6. Is it quite possibly time to stop and reboot?

Chapter 6

Optical Myopathy
Reviewing the Almighty

A God that can be understood is no God. Who can explain the Infinite in words?—W. Somerset Maugham[1]

A few years ago, my husband and I took a trip to the Sierra Nevada Mountains near Lake Tahoe. We had just purchased a new camera and wanted to try it out, so we took a gondola up to one of the mountain peaks and slowly hiked down. As we meandered through the trails, we were treated to one breathtaking vista after another. We snapped hundreds of pictures and utterly soaked in the majesty and awesomeness of God. As soon as we got back to our hotel, we downloaded the pictures so that we could share our experience with our children, who were back in Minnesota suffering through a cold winter. As each picture came up on the computer, we were increasingly disappointed. The pictures of the vast mountains and breathtaking vistas were, well, boring. Each mountain looked like the next, and nothing was terribly awe-inspiring. They looked flat, small, and manageable—nothing like what we had experienced on our hike.

So what's the difference? What's the difference between a photograph of a landscape and an actual landscape? The difference is exactly the point of this chapter. When we look at a photograph, we hold a 3 x 5 picture of a mountain in our hands. When we are standing on the top of a mountain, it is we who are indescribably held in the hand of something far bigger and more important than we could ever imagine. One of the most challenging aspects of a high-tech life is how our understanding of God moves from being unbounded and unimaginable to being sorted, definable, preprocessed, convenient, and controllable. If we aren't careful about how our technology shapes us, we may imperceptibly begin to place

109

too much importance on our own abilities to shape our environment and too little importance on the character of God. In order to better understand the choices facing us as we dial up and log in, it will be helpful to examine how our technology has changed our ways of thinking, and how in turn that thinking impacts our perception of who God is, our experience of the Christian church, and our understanding of our calling as Christians.

A New Way of Thinking

Christian Philosopher Jacques Ellul has noted the ways our thinking has changed as we move from a text-based culture to one that values images and sound bites.[2] This change can be seen in how we entertain ourselves, how we gather news, how we elect politicians, how we teach our kids, even in how we worship. Images have become just as important to us as the message; we are a culture that thinks in terms of pictures. For instance, a beautiful poem might be nice to read, but it's easy to see how it would be even more popular if beautiful images were positioned in the background. Textbooks without a lot of pictures are increasingly harder to sell. A movie probably will be more popular than the book that it's based on, and an advertisement with a color picture will be more persuasive than an ad with paragraphs of text. Although it's still important for our children to know how to read and write, media literacy is increasingly important. In the future, our children will need to know how to produce and critique images in addition to words. Even our worship services are changing as text-based liturgies and hymns filled with verse after verse of words are being replaced with moving images of flowers, crosses, or clouds that drift behind worship songs or short Scripture passages. As technology allows us to more easily manipulate and produce images, these images have become embedded in our way of thinking.

According to Ellul, this change is significant. Text allows us to think in a certain kind of way. It gives us the ability to reason abstractly, construct arguments, and create categories. It removes us from the constraints of a specific context and allows us to rationally think through big ideas. Text also changes the things we value. A society that values the written word is one that values linearity and logic. It requires that people support their claims, and it values what individuals say over what they look like. This way of thinking characterized much of our society at the turn of the last century. Can you imagine listening for hours to a political debate or a traveling preacher as people used to do? These speakers didn't even use PowerPoint! Instead, they relied on their use of language and logic to support their points and capture the attention of their audiences.

These days, if my preacher goes over the customary twenty-five minutes, I feel the itchiness in my bones. I feel trapped; my imagination begins to wander. As we have moved into an era in which images are embedded into everything we do, our thinking really has changed. Not all the changes are bad. After all, images allow us to feel things. They allow us to understand things on a more holistic and intuitive level. In a certain sense, they help us to think beyond abstract propositions and move to a more pragmatic, personalized thought life. There are, however, limitations. According to pastor Shane Hipps, "As image-based communication becomes the dominant symbol system in our culture, it not only changes the way we think but also determines what we think about. Images are not well-suited to articulate argument, categories, or abstractions. They are far better suited for presenting impressions and concrete realities."[3] As a result, we often focus on things such as personality and trustworthiness of political candidates, government officials, and even coworkers. This may substitute for our willingness to assess their ability to articulate a coherent policy position or support a relevant point. Storytelling, whether in words or images, becomes more important than specific claims or facts. "News" is just as much about what video is most sensational as it is about which story might have the most long-term significance. There's no doubt that technology has impacted how we think about things. The question then becomes "How does this change impact our understanding of an almighty God?"

A Matter of Perspective

John 1:1 puts it clearly: "In the beginning was the Word, and the Word was with God, and the Word was God." Notice that John didn't say that in the beginning was an image, or a picture, or even a story. In the beginning was the Word. Period. I'm not surprised. Scripture is full of problems that God's people have had when they try to create images of God. Even if the image is very pretty, made of glittering gold and sparkling gems, God's people create a problem when they try to capture who God is and put that into some sort of tangible, visual form. What happens is that humans have a tendency to worship the image of God instead of the reality of God. Certainly, the images help us to understand and contextualize this unmanageable concept of an almighty God. However, they also limit our understanding of a limitless God. For instance, when we see God as a shepherd, an eagle, or even a father, we better understand a particular characteristic of the Almighty. The challenge is that as we focus on the pictorial elements that we can understand and control, we may very well miss a host of other characteristics that also define an omniscient, omnipresent, omnipotent God. If we aren't careful, visual thinking can create a context-specific, world-fixed God.

Our changing way of thinking is not the only thing that can reduce our view of God. It appears that our tendency toward fragmented, superficial, self-centered relationships will somehow impact how we see and experience our Creator. I can't help but notice the way I relate with my friends and family closely resembles my interactions with God. For instance, sometimes I'm quick and just want to get down to business. It might be a couple of sentences e-mailed to a friend or a quick read through a little devotional capped off with a speedy prayer. Sometimes, it's all about me. Whether it's a self-absorbed blog or a fervent prayer that's all about meeting my needs, I find that my interpersonal relational patterns consistently transfer through to my spiritual relationship. Sometimes, I'm pretty demanding. I tell my kids what to do, and I tell God what I expect—in a nice way, of course. The thing is, God demands more. If we do nothing more with our relationship with God than we do with our relationships with others, we will miss out on the wonder, peace, and awe that result when we catch a glimpse of the Almighty. If we treat the God of the universe like anyone else on our Facebook page or e-mail list, we walk dangerously close to disrespecting our Maker. God is vastly more than something that can be fit into a schedule, stored in a database, or socially networked to friends. God is our Author and Creator. We need to make sure that we don't try to use our digital brushes to paint a pixilated portrait of a God who is infinitely far above and beyond our technology.

Another challenge to catching a view of the Almighty is the way our lives have become mediated. Life inside our air-conditioned, climate-controlled, high-def worlds takes us one step away from experiencing the bigness and the realness of things that God has created. Let me give you an example. One night, I was taking the trash down to the corner of the driveway. I like this little night-time jaunt because the neighborhood is usually quiet, no one is around, and I can just stand and look at all of the warm lights glowing inside each of the homes in our cul-de-sac. On this particular night, however, as I wheeled the trash down, there was a weird calm in the air. All of a sudden, a huge lightning crash thundered right above me. The dark sky lit up, and I swear that the crash was louder than anything I have ever experienced. I stood there with my trash in one hand, mouth wide open, gazing at the sky. My knees were wobbling as a quiet rain started falling. The first thing I thought was, "That was so cool!" My entire being was suddenly and completely encompassed, surrounded, and filled with the power of God—all while holding my trash! As I walked back into my house to finish watching *American Idol*, I felt such a disconnection. Somehow the life that had become familiar to me, the life that was highly controlled and mediated, seemed so insignificant and small compared to a life filled with real experiences and genuine wonder. There's no doubt that our mediated realities systematically reduce our understanding and experience of a huge and almighty God.

If our highly technical and mediated lives really do serve to minimize our view of God, the impact can be considerable. After all, a small God can't handle my big problems. A God who can be managed and must be worked into a schedule is one who just takes up more time in my already busy schedule. That kind of God is not life-changing and purpose-giving. And, quite honestly, that's not the kind of God I look to when I feel that things are spinning out of control. It's not the kind of God I will make sacrifices for or give my life to in a culture that tells me that it's really all about me anyway. It is not the kind of God I fear. And that can be a problem.

Whether or not we see it, feel it, or live as if it's true, God is bigger than anything we could ever hope to explain or visualize. When we take the time to step out from our mediated lives to understand and appreciate how truly great and worthy our Creator is, we can't help but be transformed. That's what "the fear of the Lord" is all about. Proverbs is quite explicit about what it means to live a life with a healthy view of the Almighty. According to Proverbs, "The fear of the LORD is the beginning of wisdom" (Proverbs 9:10); it provides a secure fortress, adds length to our lives, brings us honor, keeps us safe, and is a fountain of life. Those are exactly the things I miss out on when I live life in a way that suggests God doesn't really matter. Those are exactly the kind of things I thirst for in a high-tech, high-velocity life. How we view God really does matter.

A Matter of Worship

One of the ways we can nurture a healthy fear of the Lord and personally experience the glory of our mighty God is through the act of worship. It's no surprise that as technology challenges our understanding of the Almighty, it will also present challenges for the way we worship. Worship tends to be a highly personal experience. Whether it's singing hymns accompanied by a majestic organ and looking through stained glass windows or whispering words of praise with a small group of friends gathered around a flickering candle, our preferences and styles often dictate the way we engage in worship.

In some ways, technology truly can enhance our worship experience. At my church, I love being taken away in the whole worship encounter. The lights in the audience are turned off as the band plays and images flash across the screen. I sing, I hear, I think, and I feel adoration and devotion. One of the main reasons we started attending this church is that each week I walk in tired and stressed, and I walk out refreshed and emotionally moved. I feel that, at least for a few minutes each week, I catch a glimpse of a truly awesome God. And I'm not the only one. This megachurch reaches into the hearts of people who have never seen anything remotely beneficial to Sunday mornings. The worship style and powerful preaching have played an important role in introducing thousands of people to Jesus Christ.

As good as this new style of worship and churchgoing may be, we need to remember the axiom of media theorist Neil Postman: for everything that we gain with technology, we give something up. It's important to consider what we might be sacrificing as we move toward a kind of high-tech worship that is more visual, emotional, and sensory than logical, traditional, and message-focused. One of the possible drawbacks that I see in some of the emerging alternative worship experiences is the way the message might be confused with the experience. Shane Hipps acknowledges critics who claim that these kind of experiential, high-tech worship services "are executed with excellence and give people an experience of God but are doing little to challenge the individualistic, consumer-driven approach to faith."[4]

Sound theology and teaching are as important as ever to the church. But if Marshall McLuhan was right that the medium is the message, we may find that worship services that are more about spectacle than biblically based teaching are serving us a highly emotional form of "Christianity-lite."[5] After all, Scripture is full of complex and deeply challenging ideas, accompanied by uncomfortable and unpopular calls to commitment. In fact, sometimes the gospel is downright offensive. Living an exciting faith in a high-tech culture requires that when we engage in emotionally based worship, we need to make sure that it's accompanied by teaching that makes us think and take risks. We also need to make sure that the rough edge of the gospel is not

115

polished off in an effort to engage and emotionally satisfy a wide variety of people. Basically, we need to make sure that the medium doesn't become louder than the message. Clearly, technology can enhance our ability to worship in a way that lifts our entire spirit, but we must be aware of what we might be sacrificing every time the band amps up and the PowerPoint screen rolls down.

Another challenge related to church has to do with the problem of community. We have explored the value of community previously, but it warrants a bit more attention here. When I was growing up, we attended a very small church. They didn't have the budget for showy visual aids, no one was terribly good at playing musical instruments, and the sermons were "fine" on a good Sunday. The church still has very few technical amenities. They don't have any live feeds to powerful preaching. They don't use Facebook, they don't tweet their members, and they still have worn-out hymnbooks and King James Bibles in the pews. They lack many of the cool things that we've come to expect in a high-tech Christian culture. What they do have, however, is pretty special. They have each other. They see each other and take notice. They actually talk to new people who come in the door, and they notice when someone is missing.

By certain standards, this church is not very successful. It always lacks money, and its membership numbers are small. In many ways, however, this church is just as successful as the megachurch down the road. If we are talking about how our view of God is changed and reduced by our high-tech approach to church, then this church provides the perfect counterexample. The view of God that is extended there is less about polish and spectacle and more about a living God who reaches out through the people. It is less about beautiful pictures and feelings that flash through the worship hour and more about a powerful God who meets the real-life needs of people in unexpected and creative ways. Big and high-tech church experiences can move us and speak to the hearts of lots of people, but it's the small communities that remind us of the calling and commitment that are central to the Christian faith. No matter what size the church we attend may be, we need to find our place to fit and make sure that we don't minimize the power of the gospel or overlook the importance of community.

A Matter of Calling

The way we view an omnipotent God clearly impacts how we live out our Christianity. If our mediated and high-tech lenses limit our understanding of God, or if our worship experiences are based more on comfortable emotion and less on the uncomfortable message of the gospel, then it will come as no surprise if our lives lack the deep and fulfilling faith described in Scripture. However, if our view of God transcends the mediated experiences served to us through our technology, if it surpasses the limits of what can be preprocessed, presorted, and predicted, then we will be moved to live in ways that are countercultural, interdependent, risky, and downright exciting.

We have been created and called by God to live lives that are bigger and brighter than what most of us experience. Cultural critic Dick Staub puts it well: "Meant to be aglow with God's image, our lamp is dim, the image faded, obscured and seen through a glass darkly."[6] When we allow our culture and even our technology to define what we value, how we think, how we relate, and how we understand the almighty God, then it's not surprising that we simply blend in with everyone else. We can do better. We can make intentional choices about how we use our technology. We can be aware of what we gain and what we sacrifice every time we decide to mediate our experiences with electronic gadgets and communication devices. We can take our calling seriously.

Calling is important. Scripture defines this calling in lots of different ways, but Jesus highlighted what he considered to be the most important. He called us to first love God with all our heart, soul, and mind and then to love our neighbors as we love ourselves. In other words, as we are being transformed by a singular, focused devotion, we are called to reach out to the people whom God puts in front of us, whether it's a friend on Facebook, a coworker sitting next to us, or a child who lives on the other side of the world. And in many ways, Marshall McLuhan was right: the medium is the message. We can talk about the gospel until we are blue in the face, but until we "do" the gospel, our neighbors will hear little more than a "clanging cymbal." As we look around our world, it isn't hard to see: *we* are the medium.[7]

Why did God choose people like us? We have such a hard time focusing on anything. We run around distracted and scattered, overlooking and undervaluing others. It truly is surprising that our Creator has placed so much trust in his broken church to fulfill such a holy calling. Probably the biggest challenge that we face as we reflect on our choice and use of technology is that of how technology redefines our calling. As we have noted, we must be mindful of how our high-tech lifestyle mediates our experiences, speeds up our lives, clutters up our thinking, and disengages us from valuable relationships. If we are truly designed and created to fulfill this calling, we won't be satisfied until our entire heart, soul, and mind, and our cell phone calls, text messages, tweets, blogs, e-mails, Facebook pages, Blackberries, Bluetooth headsets, laptops, and iPods, are focused on loving God and loving others.

That's not easy! What that might look like and how that might work certainly is different for each individual. I guess it's an age-old question: How do we live in the world but not be consumed by it? How do we become tech-savvy Christians? For some, it might involve just chucking it all. Disconnecting from the tools of communication technology might equal peace and focus, real-life experiences, and rich and rewarding relationships. For others, it might mean making use of every piece of available high-tech gadgetry to intentionally engage with our culture and the people around us. In any case, we can't take our calling for granted. It doesn't just happen. As soon as we begin to thoughtlessly log on and become imperceptibly swept up in the continuous current of our cultural stream, we lose. We lose the depth, the excitement, the focus, and the realness that come when we are truly fulfilling our calling.

A Matter of Intention

It's no surprise. Things are changing and will keep changing. Life rolls along differently from the way it did in the days of Beaver Cleaver, Andy Griffith, and Lucy Ricardo. And let's face it: everyone could use a little reboot. If your Christian life needs a little technological refreshing, here are a few questions to consider every time you decide to try out a new gadget, post a new message, or text a new thought.

1. What are my choices?

   Although the benefit of your choice probably is clear, by taking some time to think about what you are giving up or what may be a better way to accomplish your goal, you may be reminded of the choices that you actually have.

2. Am I mediating an experience that needs to be experienced live?

   Whether it involves experiencing love and grief through an emotional love story in a movie, dealing with conflict between friends using Facebook or text messages, or connecting with God in ways that limit God's glory, we need to ask ourselves, "Would the experience be more effective if I removed the piece of technology sitting between me and the interaction?"

3. What am I missing?

   As we cocoon ourselves with cell phones, earbuds, and assorted hand-held devices, we clearly miss the things going on around us. Take time to pay focused attention to the person, the message, or the still, small voice that you might be missing. Look to see who is standing right there in front of you.

4. Why am I using this thing?

   In an effort to unclutter our minds and our closets, it's important to discern the difference between needs and wants. It's also important to consider when we are using something that will actually make things better and when we are using it simply because we are too lazy to do it the "right" way.

5. How will this focus my calling?

   Focus and commitment to the things that bring us closer to our stated goals are especially necessary in a culture that is overloaded and hyperdriven with information and opportunities. We need to decide how any given piece of technology will focus our lives, allowing us to love the Lord our God with our entire heart, soul, and mind and to love our neighbors as we love ourselves.

I think that Neil Postman had it right. For everything that technology gives us, it takes something away. Technology in and of itself is not evil, nor is it the answer to all our problems. It doesn't have to control us. When it comes to our faith, it's about time we grab hold of the choices that we make on a daily basis. It's about time we look at how technology is impacting our values, relationships, and faith. As difficult as it is to do, I want my life to echo what the psalmist says in Psalm 86:11–12: "Teach me your way, O LORD, and I will walk in your truth; give me an undivided heart, that I may fear your name. I will praise you, O Lord my God, with all my heart; I will glorify your name forever."

Notes

Part I: Values

1. *Wiktionary,* http://en.wiktionary.org/wiki/values (accessed September 1, 2009).

Chapter 1

1. *The Quotations Page,* http://www.quotationspage.com/quotes/ Ann_Landers (accessed September 1, 2009).
2. *You've Got Mail,* DVD, directed by Nora Ephron (Warner Home Video, 1998).
3. Quoted in Michael Bugeja, *Interpersonal Divide: The Search for Community in a Technological Age* (New York: Oxford University Press, 2005), 81.
4. Dick Staub, *The Culturally Savvy Christian: A Manifesto for Deepening Faith and Enriching Popular Culture in an Age of Christianity-lite* (San Francisco: Jossey-Bass, 2007), 7.
5. Jacques Ellul, *The Humiliation of the Word,* trans. Joyce Main Hanks (Grand Rapids: Eerdmans, 1985), 120.

Chapter 2

1. *The Quotations Page,* http://www.quotationspage.com/quotes/ Mario_Andretti (accessed September 1, 2009).
2. Richard Swenson, *The Overload Syndrome: Learning to Live within Your Limits* (Colorado Springs, CO: NavPress, 1998), 14.
3. Richard Foster, *Freedom of Simplicity: Finding Harmony in a Complex World* (San Francisco: Harper & Row, 1981), 5.
4. Swenson, *The Overload Syndrome,* 28.
5. A similar scenario can be found in ibid., 46-47.
6. Kirk Byron Jones, *Addicted to Hurry: Spiritual Strategies for Slowing Down* (Valley Forge, PA: Judson Press, 2003), 68.

Chapter 3

1. *BrainyQuote,* http://www.brainyquote.com/quotes/authors/j/jean_arp.html (accessed September 1, 2009).
2. Henri J. M. Nouwen, *The Way of the Heart: Desert Spirituality and Contemporary Ministry* (New York: Seabury Press, 1981), 45.
3. Gordon McDonald, *Ordering Your Private World* (New York: Oliver-Nelson, 1984), 14.
4. Ibid., 71.
5. Kirk Byron Jones, *Addicted to Hurry: Spiritual Strategies for Slowing Down* (Valley Forge, PA: Judson Press, 2003), 6-7.
6. Ibid., 9.
7. Richard Foster, *Freedom of Simplicity: Finding Harmony in a Complex World* (San Francisco: Harper & Row, 1981), 92.
8. McDonald, *Ordering Your Private World,* 90.
9. Nouwen, *The Way of the Heart,* 37.
10. Ibid., 32.
11. Malcolm Muggeridge, *Something Beautiful for God: Mother Teresa of Calcutta* (Garden City, NY: Image Books, 1977), 48.

Chapter 4

1. John de Gruchy, ed., *Dietrich Bonhoeffer: Witness to Jesus Christ* (Minneapolis: Fortress, 1991), 186.
2. Shane Hipps, *The Hidden Power of Electronic Culture: How Media Shapes Faith, the Gospel, and Church* (Grand Rapids: Zondervan, 2005), 111.
3. Quentin Schultz, *Habits of the High-Tech Heart: Living Virtuously in the Information Age* (Grand Rapids: Baker, 2004), 178.

Chapter 5

1. *The Quotations Page,* http://www.quotationspage.com/quote/37755.html (accessed September 1, 2009).
2. Nicole B. Ellison, Charles Steinfield, and Cliff Lampe, "The Benefits of Facebook 'Friends': Social Capital and College Students' Use of Online Social Network Sites," *Journal of*

Computer-Mediated Communication 12, no. 4, article 1 (July 2007), http://jcmc.indiana.edu/vol12/issue4/ellison.html.

3. Yifeng Hu, Jacqueline Fowler Wood, Vivian Smith, and Nalova Westbrook, "Friendships through IM: Examining the Relationship between Instant Messaging and Intimacy," *Journal of Computer-Mediated Communication* 10, no. 1, article 6 (November 2004), http://jcmc.indiana.edu/vol10/issue1/hu.html.

4. Quoted in Quentin Schultz, *Habits of the High-Tech Heart: Living Virtuously in the Information Age* (Grand Rapids: Baker, 2004), 32.

5. For more reading on hyperpersonal communication, see research done by Joseph B. Walther, such as "Computer-Mediated Communication: Impersonal, Interpersonal, and Hyperpersonal Interaction," *Communication Research* 23, no. 1 (1996): 3-43.

6. See Schultz, *Habits of the High-Tech Heart.*

7. Michael Bugeja. *Interpersonal Divide: The Search for Community in a Technological Age* (New York: Oxford University Press, 2004), 67.

8. Ibid., 69.

9. Schultz, *Habits of the High-Tech Heart,* 112.

Chapter 6

1. W. Somerset Maugham, *The Razor's Edge* (Philadelphia: Triangle Books, the Blakiston Company, 1944), 261.

2. See Jacques Ellul, *The Humiliation of the Word,* trans. Joyce Main Hanks (Grand Rapids: Eerdmans, 1985).

3. Shane Hipps, *The Hidden Power of Electronic Culture: How Media Shapes Faith, the Gospel, and Church* (Grand Rapids: Zondervan, 2005), 75.

4. Ibid., 148.

5. See Dick Staub, *The Culturally Savvy Christian: A Manifesto for Deepening Faith and Enriching Popular Culture in an Age of Christianity-lite* (San Francisco: Jossey-Bass, 2007).

6. Ibid., 50.

7. Hipps, *The Hidden Power of Electronic Culture,* 92.

Feeling Disconnected from Your Online Teen?

Get *Connected: Christian Parenting in an Age of IM and MySpace*!

"If your kids are on the Internet, this is a must-read." —David Walsh, PhD, President, National Institute on Media and the Family

Connected offers parents:
- A look at the pros and cons of online communication technology
- Ideas for how to start discussions about online communications with your children
- Real-life stories and advice from 12- to 18-year-olds who use IM and MySpace
- Advice and insight from Christian parents and experts who have dealt with teens who use online communications

Connected: Christian Parenting in an Age of IM & MySpace won a 2008 **iParenting Media Award for Outstanding Products**, and was listed as one of the **50 Best Parenting Books for Families with Tweens and Teens** by RadicalParenting.com.

978-0-8170-1516-9 $12.00

To order, call 800-458-3766 or visit www.judsonpress.com.
Save 20% when you order online!

Rewired: Youth Ministry in an Age of IM and MySpace

Peggy Kendall; Foreword by Duffy Robbins

"*I appreciate the approach taken in this book because it is thoughtful and measured—not too 'gee whiz' and not too jihad. Peggy Kendall talks about both the dangers and the benefits of cyber-relationships.*"
—Duffy Robbins, professor of youth ministry, Eastern University

Whether you're a cyberspace rookie or a social networking technology pro, *Rewired* presents food for thought and practical resources related to IM, MySpace, Facebook, and YouTube, including:

- A reader-friendly summary of research on today's online communication technology
- Insight into how these technologies affect relationships and communication
- The pros and cons of using computer-mediated communication in youth ministry
- Real-life insight and feedback from teens and youth leaders who regularly use IM and social networking
- Specific tips on IM and social networking use

978-0-8170-1513-8 $12.00

To order, call 800-458-3766 or visit www.judsonpress.com.
Save 20% when you order online!

JUDSON PRESS
PUBLISHERS SINCE 1824